Praise for *The Low-*

"Fresh and flavorful low-alcohol re_____
with heaps of artful inspiration and tips _____ ____ your own low-proof
home bar. Jules is the craft cocktail queen!"
—MARANDA PLEASANT, editor of
Thrive, Mantra Wellness, ORIGIN magazines

"Once again, I am completely gobsmacked by the creativity of
Jules Aron's cocktail recipes. . . . If there is anyone who can convince
me to tone down the booze in my drink, it's [her]."
—KATE E. RICHARDS, author of *Drinking with Chickens*

"Jules Aron takes the guessing game out of low-ABV cocktails. From bitter
liqueurs to fortified wines and everything in between, she explores the
romance of cocktails in an easily consumable way."
—GABE F. URRUTIA, author of *Miami Cocktails*

"Jules Aron has been a trusted educator incorporating wellness and
holistic practices to beverage concepts for years, and this book is a must
for both studied enthusiasts and newcomer novices."
—TARA FOUGNER, founder of Thirstymag.com

"Cheers to this fun and approachable guide to low-proof cocktails,
highlighting delicious, fresh, and natural ingredients on every page!"
—NATALIE MIGLIARINI, author of *Beautiful Booze*

"Laid out simply, elegantly, and structurally, I felt absolutely confident that
I could make the recipes [Jules] prepares. But even more importantly, as
a whiskey drinker, I found a good reason to enjoy low-ABV cocktails with
real ingredients. . . . And I can have more than one."
—ROBIN ROBINSON, author of *The Complete Whiskey Course*

"Why limit yourself to club soda and bitters when you can have cocktails
meticulously crafted and full of flavor? Now you have no excuse not to
keep celebrations going all day, every day!"
—GIOVANNI GUTIERREZ, founder *Chat Chow TV*

the low-proof
HAPPY HOUR

Real Cocktails
Without the Hangover

JULES ARON

The Countryman Press
A Division of W. W. Norton & Company
Independent Publishers Since 1923

For information about permission to reproduce selections from this book, write to
Permissions, The Countryman Press, 500 Fifth Avenue, New York, NY 10110

For information about special discounts for bulk purchases, please contact
W. W. Norton Special Sales at specialsales@wwnorton.com or 800-233-4830

Manufacturing by Versa Press
Book design by Allison Chi
Production manager: Devon Zahn

Library of Congress Cataloging-in-Publication Data

Names: Aron, Jules, author.
Title: The low-proof happy hour : real cocktails without the hangover / Jules Aron.
Description: New York, NY : The Countryman Press, a Division of W. W. Norton & Company
Independent Publishers Since 1923, [2021] |
Includes bibliographical references and index.
Identifiers: LCCN 2020037767 | ISBN 9781682685297 (pbk.) |
ISBN 9781682685303 (epub)
Subjects: LCSH: Cocktails. | LCGFT: Cookbooks.
Classification: LCC TX951 .A6764 2021 | DDC 641.87/4—dc23
LC record available at https://lccn.loc.gov/2020037767

The Countryman Press
www.countrymanpress.com

A division of W. W. Norton & Company, Inc.
500 Fifth Avenue, New York, NY 10110
www.wwnorton.com

978-1-68268-529-7 (pbk.)

10 9 8 7 6 5 4 3 2 1

To Dylan. The Zen to my Tonic.
Drinks taste best when shared with you.

contents

foreword

NATALIE MIGLIARINI | BEAUTIFUL BOOZE

I started the website Beautiful Booze in the spring of 2013 as a resource for the cocktail enthusiast and home bartender. Since then, I have had the opportunity to travel the world in search of the best cocktails. Through these global adventures, I've gained a much better understanding of the cocktail world.

One particularly difficult part of my life on the road, however, is finding a positive balance between maintaining a healthy lifestyle and enjoying the local culinary delights and nights out chasing the perfect cocktail. In my search for this balance, I discovered that low-ABV and non-alc options are becoming more sophisticated and readily available on bar menus around the world.

Only a couple of years ago, you would have been limited to sipping on sparkling water or sugary fruit juice if you wanted to enjoy a night out with little or no alcohol. However, the cocktail scene around the world has been growing and evolving, looking to cater to a new gener-ation of consumers who want more low-proof options on the menu.

Why are consumers demanding these options, you may ask? It may be because this demographic wants to maintain a healthy lifestyle and still enjoy a night out socializing without the pressure to join in on heavy drinking.

A major step forward into the psyche of offering cocktails with less alcohol is modifying the terminology we use. By simply changing the term *mocktail*—that tends to "mock" the drink and drinker—to alcohol-free or low proof, we can continue to elevate the status and experience of drinks of all kinds.

There may be many reasons for choosing low- or no-alcohol drinks, but having the option is always a plus. That's why I'm particularly delighted and honored to welcome the new book of my friend and colleague, Jules Aron. Always an inspiration in the way of holistic wellness and cleaner living, Jules has, once again, created a fun, informative new guide, this one dedicated to low-proof cocktails. And I, for one, am excited to celebrate with a couple of them.

Here's to a class of cocktails as diverse as the world. Cheers and happy drinking!

—Natalie
Beautiful Booze

introduction

There's a new buzz in cocktails and the proof is in the drink. Low-proof libations, also known as shims, suppressors, and sessions have been around for centuries. Countries like France, Italy, and Spain have enjoyed vermouth, sherry, and amaro cocktails—like the now ubiquitous spritz—for years. It seems the fever is finally spreading. Bartenders and patrons across the United States have been embracing low-alcohol libations with a new passion.

As a holistic nutritionist and longtime industry professional, I am right there with them. I'm fascinated by the historic context of medicinal herbs and botanicals and their relation to cocktails. And I am always interested in reinventing classics with fresh, seasonal ingredients in both inventive and accessible ways.

My first book, *Zen and Tonic*, was all about maximizing nutrition, flavor, and balance in plant-powered drinks. Favoring superfoods and nutrient-dense fruits, berries, and botanicals and minimizing sugar content, the book emphasized the restorative and medicinal properties of plants and botanicals in the creation of delicious spirits. Since the release of *Zen and Tonic* in 2016, the trend toward health and wellness has continued to blossom, leading me, naturally, to low-proof cocktails.

Low-alcohol drinks that contain up to 10% ABV (alcohol by volume, or 20 proof), pack all the flavor without the punch, and make it easy for folks to embrace a healthy lifestyle and stay on track with their fitness and wellness goals while still enjoying a night out with friends. Though these drinks are lightweights compared to their high-proof counterparts, they do not sacrifice flavor. In all my recipes, I continue to favor fresh fruits, veggies, and botanicals to build flavor profiles and natural sweeteners instead of refined sugars.

This book is written for you, the home bartender, so you can discover new ways of building cocktails that keep things interesting yet easy. Here, you will find a celebration of more than 100 recipes and supporting recipes that won't interfere with your wellness journey. These drinks are great for brunch and casual day drinking, and perfect for social gatherings where you're more likely to have more than one drink. And I am always mindful of keeping the recipes simple, only calling on a few bottles at a time. The recipes also allow you to discover new spirits on your own, with artisanal spirit maker spotlights throughout the book. But why stop there? "Less is more" can become your mantra to live by in more ways than one. From low alcohol to low waste, I'm always at the ready with advice to help you live your best low-proof life.

I am also inspired by this new generation of bartenders, and one of the most enjoyable aspects of creating this new book has been collaborating with some of the nation's best cocktail makers to share their take on the low-proof cocktail. I hope the recipes delight you as much as they have me.

My overall hope is that the drinks described within these pages engage all five senses and ignite your own creativity. I encourage you to experiment with various measurements, because your palate is personal to you. By playing with new flavors and mixing spirits in new ways, I hope you find your own direction into this exciting world of low-proof cocktails.

THE ANATOMY OF A LOW-PROOF COCKTAIL

A standard cocktail is made up of three principal ingredients: the base alcohol, the body or modifier, and the flavoring agent, which is also known as the perfume.

In the case of a low-proof cocktail, we maintain this balance, albeit with much less boozy proportions. Here are some general tips to get you started:

- For base ingredients, use lower-proof alcohol such as beer, wine, sake, and shochu; fortified wines such as vermouth and sherry; herbal and sweet liqueurs; and bitter amari.
- Think of strong spirits as seasoning by keeping the high-proof alcohol component to a maximum of 1 ounce.
- Build flavor, depth, and complexity with additional ingredients such as tea, spices, and botanicals.
- Maintain balance with the following three to four flavor components: alcohol, sweet, sour, and/or bitter.

TECHNIQUES

Mixing a cocktail serves three main goals: to properly blend the ingredients, to chill the drink to its ideal temperature, and to dilute the drink to a proper level. Here are some techniques to help you be a more efficient home bartender.

HOW TO SHAKE: Put your ingredients into your shaker, and fill it two-thirds of the way up with ice. Cover and shake for 12 seconds to achieve thermal equilibrium—the coldest your drink can get.

Dry Shaking: When shaking a cocktail that contains egg, cream, or aquafaba (chickpea water), a dry shake—done without ice—is required in order for the ingredients to be emulsified. Add all the ingredients into a shaker and vigorously shake for 30 seconds before adding ice and shaking once more. Double strain.

HOW TO STIR: Fill a mixing glass two-thirds with ice and add the ingredients. Holding the bar spoon with your thumb and first two fingers, place the bar spoon along the inside of the glass and gently rotate it around the outer edges.

SHAKING VS STIRRING

Shaking with ice creates air bubbles that allows nonalcoholic ingredients to blend with your spirits more easily. This technique also gives cocktails body and texture. When the recipe calls for distilled spirits only, you'll want to stir its ingredients instead.

HOW TO MUDDLE: Using the bottom of a muddler or spoon, press and extract the essence of fruits, vegetables, and other botanicals.

HOW TO RINSE: This is a helpful technique to add extra flavor, especially in low-proof drinks. Use a strong ingredient to coat or rinse the inside of a cocktail vessel. Once the glass is coated, pour out the excess liquid. Then fill the glass and enjoy your drink!

DRINKS WITH BENEFITS

Historically, humans have used almost every fruit, plant, or grain with any sugar or starch in it for the production of alcohol. The process of fermentation yielded more than alcohol. Yeasts produced vital nutrients, including niacin, riboflavin, thiamine, and folic acid, which people used to sustain themselves. In fact, in ancient Chinese medicine, most herbal prescriptions and medicine were based on alcoholic remedies and, even at the time, warned folks of potential side effects and abuse.

HOW TO FLAME: Squeeze the zest of a citrus fruit over a lit flame to caramelize the oils and add an additional aromatic element to your finished drink.

HOW TO SMOKE: Using a handheld smoker, you can experiment with adding smoky elements to your syrups, infusions, and garnishes.

OTHER SOUND COCKTAIL PRINCIPLES

Better drinks start with better ingredients. I talk extensively about organic ingredients and quality spirits in my first book, *Zen and Tonic*. Here, I share a few key principles to help your home bar creations shine, all while making small, sustainable changes to the way you buy and use ingredients.

REFUSE REFINED: As with food, fresh is best. Always use fresh pressed juices, natural sweeteners, and homemade syrups.

LOCAL AND SEASONAL: Sustainable farmer's market ingredients ensure the freshest taste with little environmental impact.

WASTE NOT—REUSE, REDUCE, RECYCLE: There are so many creative ways to use all of your produce, whether it's making a syrup with your mint stems or an infusion with your citrus rinds. For more inspiration, don't miss the sustainability tips on page 17.

NOTES ON USING THIS BOOK

You'll find a lot of advice peppered throughout this book. Keep your eye out for the following spotlights and sidebars, which are intended to honor cocktail experts, provide exciting drink variations, highlight delicious products, and give quick tips for the healthiest happy hour possible.

BREAK THE ICE—MAKER'S SPOTLIGHT—HIGHLIGHTING SMALL BATCH, ARTISANAL LIQUOR BRANDS: Because no drink can ever rise above the quality of its ingredients, you'll find small-batch, organic, and/or artisanal producers showcased throughout the book. These makers work hard to avoid artificial additives, help promote sustainable practices, and/or use environmentally friendly packaging.

Note: Additional high-quality products are listed in the Low-ABV Bottles to Know section at the back of the book.

MIX IT UP—RECIPE VARIATIONS: The Mix It Up tips throughout the book are meant to offer you additional inspiration and opportunities to riff on a particular cocktail. Whether by swapping out the indicated alcohol or by changing the flavor profile with fresh ingredient suggestions, these tips let you get the most mileage out of the recipes, as well as allow you to experiment with your own preferences.

BOTTLE SPOTLIGHT: Bottle Spotlights offer additional discussions and clarifications on ingredients and products used in any given recipe. They are meant to help you understand why a certain bottle is used in a recipe, and they offer up additional suggestions and inspiration for further experimentation.

DRINKS WITH BENEFITS—NUTRITIONAL SPOTLIGHTS: Drinks with Benefits is a reference taken from my previous book *Zen and Tonic*, which was sprinkled with nutritional spotlights. I continue the tradition here by featuring and spotlighting healthy ingredients used throughout the book.

WASTE NOT: GENERAL SUSTAINABILITY TIPS

The following tips are meant to inspire thoughtful usage of ingredients and positive, environmentally friendly lifestyle changes. The journey toward sustainability can be full of challenges. But there's no need to take on more than you can handle. Small, conscious actions are impactful, and it's their combined effect that creates lasting change.

- Choose package-free or bulk items.
- Carry reusable bags.
- Use cloth napkins instead of paper towels.
- Store food in glass or metal containers instead of sealable plastic bags and plastic wrap.
- Peel your citrus before juicing them and reserve the peel for using in cordials and tonic syrups.
- Use carrot and strawberry tops to make infusions, and dehydrate wilted herbs to use as garnishes and seasonings.
- Leftover herbs can be sun-dried and ground to be used in flavored salts. You can also freeze a mixture of herbs in ice cube trays to prepare frozen herb cubes. Finally, save your mint, cilantro, rosemary, and thyme stems for infusions.
- Spring onions, celery, fennel, coriander, beet, and leek roots make great additions to your kitchen garden. Simply cover the base of these vegetables in water and leave them in the sun. Sprouts should appear within days.
- Save the tops of pineapples to regrow new ones. Pits of plums, peaches, and avocados can also be planted.
- Keep plant-based scraps such as fruits and vegetables, as well as grains, nuts, coffee, grinds, and tea bags, in a small stainless steel container in the freezer that you can take to your local farmers' market to compost.
- Tea bags often contain plastic that prevents the paper from dissolving in boiling water. Use loose-leaf tea and a metal strainer instead. You can also compost the tea leaves.

a guide to LOW-PROOF ALCOHOL

The recipes in this book call predominantly for low-proof bottles. If you're used to mixing up martinis and manhattans for dinner parties, then you're already familiar with some of the low-proof alcohols referred to in this section. Either way, this is an exciting category to explore.

LIQUEURS | ABV RANGE: 15 TO 30%

Liqueurs are distilled spirits that have been flavored and sweetened with a variety of fruits, herbs, flowers, or nuts. These generally contain 15 to 30% ABV (but can be as high as 55%) and can be further classified into three distinct categories.

FRUIT AND FLORAL LIQUEURS: This category has been recently reinvigorated with fresh, new takes on what used to be sickly sweet and syrupy liqueurs. Look for high-end products made with fresh, natural ingredients, such as Giffard, Combier, and Leopold Bros.

HERBAL LIQUEURS: Liqueurs in this category are flavored primarily with herbs and roots. Examples include Chartreuse, made by the Carthusian monks for centuries, and gentian-flavored Suze and Salers.

BITTER LIQUEURS: Often associated with a specific region, bitter liqueurs (*amari* is the Italian word for "bitter"), range from mildly bitter, like the popular Aperol (from Padua, Italy) to the highly bitter and herbaceous ones, such as Martini Riserva Speciale from Turin. Other amari are characterized by one main flavor, like the artichoke-based Cynar, the citrus-forward Averna, or the minty and bitter Fernet-Branca, while others like Montenegro include a list of 40 ingredients.

WINES | ABV RANGE: 5 TO 15%

There are nine categories of wine, the most common being sparkling, white, red, rosé, and dessert. On average, these contain 11 to 13% alcohol, making them a versatile ingredient when building low-ABV cocktails.

FORTIFIED AND AROMATIZED WINES | ABV RANGE: 16 TO 24%

A fortified wine is defined as a wine with an added distilled spirit that increases its alcohol content, hence, strengthening or fortifying it. Both vermouth and sherry are fortified wines. Alcohol content in fortified wines ranges between 17 and 20%.

SHERRY: Named after the town of Jerez de la Frontera (in Spain), sherry (or jerez) is a fortified wine from selected grapes of a specific terroir that are aged in oak. There are four dry and two sweet sherry styles. Dry styles of sherry, such as fino and Manzanilla, are aged for at least 2 years, making for their light, dry, and saline quality. Amontillado starts off as a fino but is exposed to air during its aging process, resulting in a deeper colored, rich, and nutty-flavored sherry. The sweet styles include Palo Cortado, which is rich and elegant, and oloroso, which is fortified to 17% and is dark, sweet, and robust.

VERMOUTH: Vermouth is a fortified, aromatized wine that was originally formulated as a medicinal tonic by herbalist Antonio Benedetto Carpano in 1786. Although you might only know it for its use in martinis and manhattans, vermouth is a complex spirit that can stand on its own.

Vermouth is made by adding a neutral spirit to wine and infusing it with a blend of herbs, spices, barks, and fruits. There are three primary styles of vermouth: red or sweet, dry, and blanc or bianco. Sweet vermouth originated in Turin, Italy, in the late 18th century and is a dark color with sweet spice notes. Dry vermouth, originally from Marseille, France, and blanc vermouth from Chambéry, France, are both clear and herbaceous, with the latter being sweeter.

FORTIFIED WINES

When it comes to fortified wine types, there's a significant range of classifications to explore. For example, vermouth belongs to a subcategory of fortified wine known as aromatized wine, defined as flavored with herbs, spices, and/or other natural ingredients. As with wines, both vermouth and sherry oxidize quickly once opened and so should be corked and refrigerated.

BEER | ABV RANGE: 3 TO 13%

With over 3,000 craft breweries in the United States alone, the world of beers is vast and complex. For starters, you can classify all beers as lagers or ales, depending on the type of yeast used during the fermentation process. Ales are made with yeast that ferments at the top. Lagers have yeast that ferments at the bottom of the beer mixture.

Examples of ales include brown ale, pale ale, India pale ale (IPA), English-style pale ale (ESB), porter, stout, Belgian-style beer, and wheat beer.

Examples of lagers include pale lagers and pilsners, dark lagers, and German-style bocks.

There are also spontaneously fermenting yeasts, which make wild or sour ales such as American sour beer and Belgian fruit lambic.

HARD CIDER | ABV RANGE: 1.2% TO 8.5%

Made from the fermented juice of apples with a balance of acidity, sugar, and tannin, ciders range in taste from sweet to sour and funky, depending on where they are produced. Sparkling ciders are fine with persistent bubbles; pétillant ciders have small, subtle bubbles; and ice cider is frozen before fermenting into cider. Note: Not all cider has bubbles—there's a whole category of still ciders with no carbonation.

SAKE | ABV RANGE: 15% TO 16%

A Japanese wine made from polished rice grains that undergo a brewing process. Just like wine, sake can be dry or sweet and makes for a fun cocktail base for lighter drinks.

SHOCHU | ABV RANGE: 20% TO 35%

Shochu is a single-distilled liquor made from sweet potato, barley, or rice. It retains the characteristics of its base ingredient and is worth exploring. Look for honkaku shochu (top quality).

HIGH-PROOF SPIRITS | ABV RANGE 36% TO 95%

Typical high-proof alcohols such as vodka, gin, rum, whiskey, and tequila are used to add depth and flavor to your low-ABV drinks. The idea is to keep the strong spirit under ¾ ounce in low-proof cocktails, using them to season drinks instead.

Vodka 40% to 95%   Whiskey 36% to 50%
Gin 36% to 50%   Tequila 50% to 51%
Rum 36% to 50%

stocking your LOW-PROOF BAR

Stocking your home bar should be a fun and exciting venture. If you own my first cocktail book, *Zen and Tonic*, you're already in good shape. As with that book, I've kept my suggestions here accessible, affordable, and simple for any budding home bar enthusiast.

This section provides a list of the essential bar and kitchen equipment you'll need, as well as glassware to get you started. It also covers the fundamentals of ice, garnishes, and everything you need to know about natural sweeteners and homemade infusions.

If you have difficulty finding some extras, consult the resources section at the back of the book (page 221). It contains a list of websites to help you source extras you might not find locally.

ESSENTIAL TOOLS

The first step to making a great cocktail is to have the necessary tools at hand. While it is perfectly possible to improvise with kitchen tools you already own, a few key pieces of inexpensive equipment can elevate the experience and make it that much more fun and easy.

BAR SPOON: A long-handled metal spoon with a spiral handle. It is used for stirring, scooping, and layering all your future drinks.

MIXING TIN/SHAKER: There are many cocktail shaker styles on the market, but the one I always recommend is the tried-and-true Boston Shaker. It consists of a pint-sized mixing glass and a slightly larger tin that fits over it. The glass half can be used for mixing stirred drinks as well.

JIGGER: A two-sided hourglass-shaped stainless steel measurement tool. It features a standard shot measurement, or jigger, on one end (2 ounces) and a thimble or pony shot measurement on the other (1 ounce). It also features graduated marks on the inside for ¼, ½, and ¾ ounce.

MUDDLER: A sturdy tool, similar to a pestle, that is used to press and extract flavors from fruit and herbs.

STRAINER, HAWTHORNE OR MESH: The Hawthorne strainer is an all-purpose strainer with a circular coil around the edges. The strainer, when placed over the shaker, separates ice and muddled particles out of your finished drinks. Mesh strainers are used in conjunction with the Hawthorne to double-strain smaller particles.

ADDITIONAL TOOLS

Knife and cutting board
Blender
Citrus juicer
Y-peeler

Microplane grater
Pots and pans
Mason jars and bottles
Ice cube trays

WASTE NOT: STRAWS THAT DON'T SUCK

In the United States alone, an average of 220 million straws are used each day. Here are a few alternatives:

PAPER: These are compostable, biodegradable, and made from renewable resources.

BAMBOO: These straws have a low carbon footprint and have a sustainable production process. They are usually made without pesticides or dye and are compostable.

GLASS: These straws are best with drinks that have high acidity. They are not very biodegradable.

METAL: The most common reusable straw, it is easy to clean and compact. Keep in mind that metal straws transfer heat easily.

SILICONE: Although hard to recycle, the production of silicone straws produces nine times less greenhouse gases than plastic straws.

EDIBLE: These straws are edible, biodegradable, and have a low carbon footprint.

NO STRAW: The cheapest and most sustainable option is to skip the straw altogether. If you have the option to go strawless, choose it.

RAISING A GLASS: GUIDE TO GLASSWARE

The shape of a glass affects a drink's look, smell, taste, and temperature. Stemware is designed to keep fingers from warming up the glass. The wider the mouth, the more the drink comes in contact with oxygen, which affects the taste. The narrow nozzle of champagne flutes keeps champagne sparkling, while champagne coupes and martini glasses keep the ingredients from separating. To keep things simple, I suggest you narrow down your glassware to five essentials.

THE COLLINS OR HIGHBALL GLASS (8 TO 12 OUNCES): For fizzes, mules, and other carbonated drinks.

THE OLD-FASHIONED OR ROCKS GLASS (6 TO 8 OUNCES): A versatile glass used for negronis, old-fashioneds, and other drinks served over ice.

THE CHAMPAGNE FLUTE: For kir royales, bellinis, mimosas, and champagne cocktails.

THE CHAMPAGNE COUPE (4 TO 6 OUNCES): For champagne cocktails, daiquiris, martinis, and other cocktails served up.

THE WINE STEM: For spritzes, sangrias, and punches.

Other cocktail glass styles to know include the pint glass, punch cup, Irish coffee glass, tiki mug, copper mule mug, mint julep cup, gin balloon, snifter, and the Nick and Nora glass. These are great to have on hand but not necessary for any of the cocktails in this book.

GETTING CLEAR ON ICE

Ice serves two purposes in cocktail making. Firstly, it chills the cocktail while shaking or stirring, while also diluting the drink ever so slightly to drinking perfection. Secondly, it keeps the finished cocktail chilled while you enjoy it. As an alternative to water, try making ice using fresh-squeezed juices. Simply add the juice ice to water, soda, and spirits.

The type of ice you use when shaking and serving also dramatically affects your drink.

ICE CUBES: These are used when you want to keep your drink cold without diluting it. Fresh, large cubes between 1 and 2 inches work best. The larger the cube, the slower the melting process.

CRUSHED ICE: This type of ice is used in stronger cocktails that are meant to be diluted. To make your own, place ice cubes in a blender or food processor and set the machine on the PULSE setting. Pulse in 3-second spurts for about 1 minute. You can also fold ice in a clean tea towel and use a large rolling pin to crush your ice manually.

MOLDS: Using fun-shaped molds can add interest to any drink.

PUNCH WREATHS: Fill a Bundt cake pan with distilled water, citrus wheels, and an assortment of berries, and then freeze it. Place the ice wreath in the center of a filled punch bowl to cool and add flavor to the punch as the ice melts.

FLAVORED ICE CUBES

Flavored ice cubes are like jewelry for your drink—eye-catching and loaded with personality. They're also functional: As the cubes melt, they add hints of flavor, turning even a plain glass of water into an aromatic sip. See Supporting Recipes (page 187) for ice cube recipes.

CLEAR ICE CUBES

Ice is only as good as the water used to make it. Consider using filtered water, spring water, or boiled water to remove cloudiness.

cocktail pantry BASICS

When it comes to cocktails, flavor, freshness, and seasonality are essential. A pantry stocked with fresh staples ensures you have what you need to create a delicious array of low-proof cocktails from this book and beyond.

BITTERS, SYRUPS, AND BEYOND

Just as salt and pepper are vital seasonings in cooking, so too are the following ingredients vital for balancing flavor in cocktails.

BITTERS: Created originally as cure-all tonics, bitters are now a common ingredient found in most bars. Like seasoning, bitters add aromatic complexity to cocktails. They are essentially liquid extracts of various fruits, vegetables, roots, barks, herbs, spices, and botanicals with an added "bittering agent," such as gentian root, quassia bark, burdock root, hops, chinchona bark, dandelion root, and/or citrus peels. Many artisanal bitters are on the market these days. You can also make your own (see Supporting Recipes on page 187).

SYRUPS: Cocktails made with infused syrups add a complexity and depth that you can taste. Possibilities include an extra hint of cinnamon, a floral undertone, a prick of heat, a fresh hint of mint. Best of all, these infusions are simple to create. They just take a little time and some forethought. For recipes and inspiration, see Supporting Recipes (page 187).

THE SWEET SPOT: HEALTHIER ALTERNATIVES TO REFINED SUGAR SYRUPS

Sweetness is a key component to any good drink, helping balance acid, bitterness, and even alcohol. Swap your regular simple syrup and processed sugars for these natural ones for a healthy dose of sweet nutrients. Following is my recommended list of natural sweeteners to keep your drinks naturally sweet.

Some alternative sweeteners to explore include:

Raw honey

Maple syrup

Brown rice syrup

Coconut sugar

Date Syrup (page 190)

Blackstrap Molasses Syrup (page 188)

Yacon syrup

Monk fruit

Choose sweeteners that contain no additives, little processing, and have added health benefits.

ALCOHOL INFUSIONS: Infusing spirits with flavor is a great way to experiment with your own personal tastes. The basic concept is to marry a variety of choice flavors into a base liquor to create a custom-flavored spirit. You can give your spirit a subtle hint of spice or deep, aromatic notes of flavor simply by choosing how long you let your infusion sit.

Follow these guidelines for best results:

- Strong flavors such as hot peppers, vanilla pods, and lavender flowers only need a few hours to a day.
- Fresh herbs, ginger, and citrus peels need 1 to 3 days, tops.
- Most fruits and berries need 3 to 6 days.
- Vegetables and hardy fruits like apples and pears need 5 to 7 days.

DRINK WITH BENEFITS

While Hippocrates may be known as the father of medicine, it is the teachings of Galen, a 2nd-century Greek physician, that introduced us to the concept of infusing spirits with medicinal plants. The mixture of water and alcohol allowed for the dissolution of water-soluble and alcohol-soluble plant particles creating powerful medicinal elixirs. In fact, many of today's spirits such as Vermouth, Chartreuse, and Benedictine were designed as health elixirs and stomach tonics.

Head to the resource section for infusions used in the recipes of this book. For more on infusions and for dozens of additional recipes, please refer to my first cocktail book, *Zen and Tonic*. Other infusions can be made using vinegar and oil to boost the flavor and aromatics of your cocktails.

SHRUBS: Also known as a drinking vinegar, shrubs became popular during America's colonial era. Besides being an excellent preservative, vinegar is also great for extracting minerals. The sweet and sour combination provides balance and complexity to drinks. While any vinegar can be used in making a shrub, champagne vinegar, apple cider vinegar, and balsamic vinegar work great.

FRESH PRESSED JUICES: Fresh is best. Always have fresh citrus fruit on hand for a quick press: lemon, lime, and grapefruit are classics. Berries, stone fruits, and melons can be muddled right into drinks. Other fruit can be juiced or blended and strained for the best flavor.

Citrus peels can be used for twists, infusions, and an oleosaccharum (oily sugar), which is a 19th-century recipe for adding sweetness, flavor, and aromatics to cocktails. Simply muddle the sugar and citrus peels until they release the fragrant oils. Such concoctions are often used in punches but are equally delicious in single-serve cocktails, ice cream, and even pancakes.

PLANT-BASED MILKS: Nut milks, oat milk, and coconut milk are great when a creamy texture is needed. Plus, they are easy to work with. See my recipe for homemade Oat Milk on page 211.

KOMBUCHA: Want a little probiotic kick with your fizzy drink? Kombucha and other probiotic waters can replace your seltzer and other bubbles.

CHICKPEA WATER (AQUAFABA): The water from canned chickpeas and other beans have an emulsifying and thickening action. They make a great vegan alternative to egg whites.

ESSENTIAL OILS: Edible-grade oils add complexity, flavor, scent, and medicinal properties of your favorite plants to your drinks. Just be mindful, a drop or two is usually all you need.

CITRIC ACID: Citric acid is used to increase the shelf life of low- and no-alcohol infusions and syrups, as well as a low level of acidity. It can be sourced in powdered form from a natural food store or online.

PLANTS AND BOTANICALS

HERBS AND SPICES

Let the seasons guide you in creating drinks with benefits! Once you discover the fresh, flavorful magic of herbs and spices that are at their peak, you'll never turn back. Just as with fruit and vegetables, it's about finding delicious, organic, and ethically and locally sourced ingredients whenever possible. Just refer to this handy list for a rundown of herbal health benefits.

BASIL: Antiaging, anti-inflammatory

BLACK PEPPERCORN: Aids in nutrient absorption, increases metabolism

CARDAMOM: Promotes heart health, digestive aid

CAYENNE PEPPER: Reduces inflammation, boosts metabolism

CHILI POWDER: Regulates blood pressure, reduces pain

CILANTRO: Soothes sore throat, speeds digestion

CINNAMON: Helps control blood sugar, reduces bad cholesterol

DILL: Helps control levels of blood cholesterol, natural antioxidant

GARLIC: Protects against heart disease, antibacterial, antiviral

GINGER: Aids digestion, soothes upset stomach, anti-inflammatory

MUSTARD: Improves circulation, relieves congestion

OREGANO: Antibacterial, antifungal, reduces inflammation

PARSLEY: Calms nerves, natural antioxidant

ROSEMARY: Improves digestion, enhances concentration

SEA SALT: Offers trace minerals (which are processed out of table salt)

THYME: Reduces inflammation, controls blood pressure

TURMERIC: Regulates hormones, boosts metabolism, anti-inflammatory

WASABI: Improves circulation, boosts metabolism

EDIBLE FLOWERS

Flowers have long been used in natural remedies and homeopathic health treatments. The culinary use of flowers dates back thousands of years to the ancient Chinese, Greek, and Roman cultures. If nothing else, flowers add color, flavor, and whimsy to your cocktails. They can also make the prettiest ice cubes (recipe on page 200). Here is a detailed list of some flowers that can lend extra oomph to your drinks.

CHAMOMILE: Chamomile's slightly earthy, sweet flavor is often used to make tea or other infusions. They are often used medicinally to reduce anxiety and improve sleep.

DANDELION: Dandelions are a highly nutritious edible flower with incredible detoxifying benefits that help restore hydration and electrolyte balance.

HIBISCUS: Hibiscus flowers are large, colorful blooms that grow in tropical climates. The flowers can be eaten raw and are often brewed into a beautiful crimson tea. Hibiscus is rich in antioxidants and is known for lowering blood pressure.

HONEYSUCKLE: A fragrant flower with a sweet flavor and distinct aroma. It is used in traditional medicine to treat digestive issues, respiratory conditions, and viral and bacterial infections.

LAVENDER: A violet flower with a distinct aroma. It may be eaten fresh or dried and has been used to treat nausea, anxiety, and insomnia.

MARIGOLD: Marigolds, also known as calendula, are often used as topical skin remedies. They are also a rich source of flavonoid, which promotes cell health and lutein, which helps prevent degenerative eye conditions.

NASTURTIUM: A brightly colored flower with a savory, peppery bite. Both the flowers and leaves contain high levels of vitamin C with immune-boosting benefits. It can be prepared in a variety of ways.

PANSY: Pansies make a colorful and nutritious addition to your drinks. They are a rich source of potent plant compounds and contain antioxidant and anti-inflammatory properties.

ROSE: Delicate and fragrant, rose petals and rose hips have been used for health in various ways. They are rich in antioxidants and contain high amounts of vitamins A and E. The ancient Chinese used it to treat digestive and menstrual concerns.

VIOLET: This small flower packs a nutritional punch. Violets not only hold anti-inflammatory properties, they are also potassium-rich, helping heart and muscle function. They also contain rutin, which boosts blood vessel health.

TEA

With its essential tannins, bitter flavors, and floral notes, tea has played an important role in cocktails since the days of the 17th-century punch.

Derived from the *Camellia sinensis* plant, native to China and India, the tea contains antioxidants called flavonoids, including the

HOW TO BREW A PROPER CUP OF TEA

From classic greens to roasted teas, and more delicate blends, water temperature is at the core of your flavor experience. Here's how to brew your most loved types of tea.

TEA	TEMPERATURE	AMOUNT	STEEPING TIME
Black	200 to 205°F	1 teaspoon	3 to 5 minutes
Green	175 to 180°F	1 teaspoon	3 minutes
Blends	190 to 205°F	1 teaspoon	3 minutes
Matcha	175°F	1½ teaspoons	whisk for 10 seconds
Herbal	205°F	1 tablespoon	5 minutes
Oolong	185 to 205°F	1 teaspoon	3 to 5 minutes
Pu-erh	195 to 205°F	1 tablespoon	3 to 5 minutes
White	175 to 185°F	1 tablespoon	1 to 3 minutes

powerful EGCG (epigallocatechin gallate), that help protect against free radicals.

THE 101 ON GARNISHES

Besides adding a decorative touch to your drink, garnishes should also provide integral, complementary flavors and aromas. A strategically placed citrus peel on the side of a drink that a guest can rub and squeeze will release just a touch of aroma to stimulate the senses. Edible flowers, fruit, berries, and other botanical ingredients can be wedged between ice cubes and the glass to create an overall sensory impact. But remember: Whether they're simple or elaborate, garnishes should never take away from the drink itself. Select them in order to complement the texture, color, and taste of the drink. And of course, they should always be edible!

CITRUS TWISTS: Cut the ends of your citrus fruit and make an incision halfway through the fruit lengthwise. Using your thumb, separate the rind from the meat of your citrus fruit until you have removed the entire skin. Roll up the whole skin and cut into pieces to make curly twists.

FANS: You can make attractive edible fans using pears, apples, and strawberries. Simply pick a fruit with firm flesh. Slice the fruit very thinly, leaving a tail at the bottom. Spread the slices out in a fan shape. Make sure to soak the fruit in lemon juice to prevent it from browning.

FRESH HERB SPRIGS: Adding a fresh herb sprig of mint, basil, rosemary, thyme, or sage has a way of elevating a simple drink to a notable experience. Before adding herbs to your cocktail, help the leaves release their aroma and flavor. For soft leafy herbs such as mint or basil, place the leaves in your palm and give it a nice firm slap. For sturdier rosemary or thyme, simply tap it on the back of your hand before placing it on the glass.

To preserve herbs, loosely wrap the bunch in a barely damp paper towel and seal that in a lidded glass container to create an environment humid enough to keep the herbs moist.

SALT OR SUGAR RIMS: Sugars and salts can be flavored with crushed flowers, herbs, and spices. Get creative! I also love to use an assortment of pink Himalayan and black Hawaiian salts, and brown and flavored sugars. You'll find that the smaller the crystals, the easier to coat the rim. For salty or savory rims, cut a slot into a wedge of lime and gently rub it around the rim of a glass before coating. For a sweet rim, do the same with a syrup.

For the following rim and garnish recipes, please refer to my previous book, *Zen and Tonic*.

Lavender Sugar Rim	Chili Salt Rim
Lemon Sugar Rim	Candied Lavender Sprigs
Rosebud Sugar Rim	Candied Rose Petals

INFUSED SALT: Dress up your margaritas by rimming them with a custom-flavored salt. Use a food processor or mortar and pestle to grind coarse salt with complementary herbs or citrus zest.

FLOAT: Try drizzling wine, juice, or bitters on top of your drink for a dramatic look and first sip experience. To do this, drizzle your float slowly over the back of a spoon into the finished drink.

DRINK WELL

Fresh ingredients, high-quality alcohol, and low-proof recipes make for a better drink experience when done in moderation. Drink well and responsibly. All the recipes in this book make one serving unless otherwise noted.

classic
COCKTAILS

The drink recipes in this chapter are historic formulas ready for riffing. Feel free to use them as templates and change them up as you desire. They are pre-Prohibition-era drinks with a whole lot of history that evoke ease and simplicity. Many of these mid-18th-century cocktails that we now call classics were made with vermouth, sherry, or wine—they're the original low-proof cocktails that continue to inspire modern interpretations.

SHERRY COBBLER `SERVES 1`

At only 16 to 18% alcohol, you simply cannot talk about low-proof cocktails without a nod to the sherry cobbler. This nearly two-centuries-old drink consists of sherry, sugar, and citrus served over crushed ice. It was popularized by author Charles Dickens when his character Chuzzlewit, of *The Life and Adventures of Martin Chuzzlewit*, described his very first sherry cobbler: "Martin took the glass with an astonished look; applied his lips to the reed; and cast up his eyes once in ecstasy. He paused no more until the goblet was drained to the last drop. . . . 'This wonderful invention, sir,' said Mark, tenderly patting the empty glass, 'is called a cobbler. Sherry cobbler when you name it long; cobbler, when you name it short.'"

---

3 orange slices

½ ounce Simple Syrup (page 188)

3½ ounces Amontillado sherry

Lemon wheel

Seasonal berries

Mint leaves

Reusable straw

ADD the orange slices and syrup to a mixing glass and gently muddle to release juices. Add the sherry and ice and shake.

STRAIN into a Collins glass filled with crushed ice.

GARNISH with the lemon wheel, seasonal berries, mint, and straw.

mix it up

PINING FOR CHAI
COBBLER SERVES 1

Sherry, sugar, and citrus meets warm chai spices and fresh pineapple slices in this flavorful sherry twist that's perfect for all seasons. The tea amplifies the natural spice notes in Amontillado sherry and brings an additional dimension to the summer drink that carries it through into the colder months.

½ ounce Chai Syrup
    (page 189)
3½ ounces
    Amontillado sherry
Pineapple slice and
    leaves
Ground nutmeg
Mint leaves
Reusable straw

ADD the syrup and sherry to a mixing glass with ice and shake.

STRAIN into a Collins glass filled with crushed ice.

CUT the pineapple slice into half-wheels. Sprinkle the drink with nutmeg and garnish with a pineapple half-wheel, pineapple leaves, mint, and straw.

Pining for Chai Cobbler

Pimm's Pop

PIMM'S CUP `SERVES 1`

The Pimm's Cup is to Wimbledon as the mint julep is to the Kentucky Derby. The original Pimm's No. 1 was created by James Pimm, a fishmonger who served the original gin-based liqueur spiked with fruit peels, herbs, and botanicals, such as quinine, to aid digestion at his popular oyster bars in London. Today, it's bottled at 25% ABV, or 50 proof.

The Pimm's Cup, typically made with cucumbers, oranges, and/or strawberries, is also ripe for variations. Try adding seasonal fruit, create a large batch for easy entertaining, or freeze them for a refreshing poptail. The following is the original Pimm's Cup recipe, followed by a modified poptail version.

Adorn your cup with fresh berries, citrus, green apple, borage, or mint and cucumber. The grander the garnish, the better.

---

2 ounces Pimm's No. 1
½ ounce lemon juice
¼ ounce Simple Syrup (page 188)
Lemon lime soda to top
Your choice of fresh fruit, cucumber, mint, etc.

ADD the Pimm's, lemon juice, and syrup to a Collins glass and stir. Add ice, top with the lemon lime soda, and stir gently to mix.

GARNISH with your choice of fresh fruit, cucumber, mint, etc.

Try adding a few dashes of bitters or substituting with ginger beer to add a little kick and complexity to the mix.

mix it up

PIMM'S POP MAKES 8–10 POPS

The quintessential Wimbledon fruit cup in a decidedly fun and frozen variation. With the traditional base of Pimm's and fruity flavors, this frozen treat gets an additional kick from the unexpected crimson peppercorn syrup.

1 cup lemon juice

2 cups ginger tea, brewed and cooled

1 cup Hibiscus & Pink Peppercorn Syrup (page 190)

1¼ cups Pimm's No. 1

1 cucumber, thinly sliced

5 strawberries, hulled and quartered

Fresh mint leaves

COMBINE the lemon juice, tea, syrup, and Pimm's in a large mixing bowl. Add a mixture of sliced cucumbers, strawberries, and fresh mint into each ice pop mold and top with the Pimm's mixture.

INSERT wooden sticks into the molds and freeze for at least 6 hours or overnight.

CLASSIC VERMOUTH COCKTAIL `SERVES 1`

Clocking in between 15% and 18% alcohol by volume, the fortified wine we know as vermouth has been an integral component in classic cocktails for centuries. But before it was mixed in martinis and manhattans, vermouth was enjoyed on its own. The iconic vermouth cocktail was made with both sweet and dry varieties, and further mixed together for countless variations. Here is a base recipe for you to explore.

2 ounces vermouth (any choice)
1 dash Angostura bitters and/or 1 dash orange bitters
Lemon twist, orange twist, or olive

ADD all the ingredients in a mixing glass with ice and then stir.

STRAIN into a chilled coupe.

EXPRESS the lemon twist or orange twist over the drink and set it on the edge of the glass, or serve with an olive.

bottle spotlight

The first commercially available vermouth, a dark and sweet variety, was made by Antonio Benedetto Carpano in Turin, Italy, in 1786. It quickly caught on with the Italian nobility and more commercial producers soon followed suit. By the beginning of the 19th century, Frenchman Joseph Noilly was producing a dry, pale variety, solidifying the general association of France with dry vermouth and Italy with sweet vermouth, although both countries eventually produced a variety of styles.

Classic Vermouth Cockail

Adonis

Bamboo

ADONIS `SERVES 1`

From punches to cobblers, both sherry and vermouth were integral parts of any 18th- and 19th-century bar menu. The 1880s saw the creation of one of the most enduring of such drinks, the Adonis. Created by the Waldorf Astoria hotel and named after the very first Broadway musical to run for more than 500 shows, this mild, easy drinking sipper, combined both sweet vermouth and sherry in equal proportions for a 12% ABV drink. It was a crowd favorite until sherry fell out of favor post-Prohibition. Thanks to the cocktail revival, this classic stirred apéritif has been rediscovered by many craft bars. Here is the original recipe.

---

2 ounces dry sherry

2 ounces sweet vermouth

2 dashes orange bitters

Orange twist

ADD the sherry, vermouth, bitters, and ice to a mixing glass. Stir until chilled.

STRAIN into a chilled coupe.

EXPRESS the orange twist over the cocktail and then drop the twist into the coupe.

BAMBOO `SERVES 1`

Also enjoying a revival, the Bamboo, at just 12% ABV, shines as a low-alcohol sipper. With no high-proof spirits, this sherry martini is made with equal parts sherry and vermouth, just like the Adonis, only replacing the sweet vermouth with the dry. This dry apéritif, created in the 1890s by Louis Eppinger at the Grand Hotel in Yokohama, Japan, quickly traveled to America, becoming one of the most famous sherry-based drinks of the 19th century. You'll find it in most craft cocktail bars these days as well.

1½ ounces dry vermouth
1½ ounces dry sherry
2 dashes orange bitters
2 dashes aromatic bitters
Orange twist

ADD the vermouth, sherry, bitters, and ice to a mixing glass. Stir until chilled.

STRAIN into a chilled coupe.

EXPRESS the orange twist over the cocktail and then drop the twist into the coupe.

bottle spotlight

Dry vermouth will add a bitter finish to this drink. You can try using a sweeter sherry or port, or substitute the dry vermouth with a blanc vermouth, for a less bitter experience.

THE CHAMPAGNE COCKTAIL **SERVES 1**

Dating back to the mid-1800s, the original champagne cocktail consisted of a chilled flute with an Angostura-soaked sugar cube topped with champagne and garnished with a lemon twist. From there, the drink blossomed to become today's favorite brunch beverage. Replace the sugar cube with OJ and it's a mimosa. Add peach puree and it's a bellini. Add a half-ounce of crème de cassis and it's a kir royale. The list of variations goes on and on!

1 sugar cube
3 or 4 dashes
   Angostura bitters
4 ounces champagne
   or dry sparkling
   wine, chilled

ADD a sugar cube to a champagne flute and dash the sugar with the bitters. Top with champagne.

The sugar cube serves to create bubbles in the glass; as such, it is best not to use loose sugar or to crush the cube.

VARIATIONS ON A THEME
While the classic champagne cocktail calls for Angostura bitters, changing up the bitters can pleasantly vary the flavor. Try experimenting with various citrus bitters for a fun twist.

For other flavor profile inspirations, try substituting orange juice for blood orange juice, peach puree for passion fruit pulp, and crème de cassis for strawberry puree. The possibilities are endless.

THE SPRITZ SERVES 1

Today's trending sparkling cocktail, the spritz, also got its start more than 150 years ago as a wine spritzer. Wines were first diluted with a splash, or *spritzen* in German, of water, then bubbly water, and then by adding fortified wines and liqueurs. The spritz follows a simple formula. Learn it and you'll have endless variations to choose from.

THE 3-2-1 SPRITZ MATRIX
3 parts sparkling wine
2 parts bitter liqueur
1 splash soda water
Orange slice or twist

ADD the sparkling wine, liqueur, and soda water into a wine stem filled with ice and stir gently.

GARNISH with an orange slice or twist.

bottle spotlight

Any number of bitter apéritifs can be used in a spritz, including Aperol, Campari, Punt e Mes, Cappelletti, Cynar, and Gran Classico, just to name a few.

THE BEER COCKTAIL

The beer cocktail has a long and rich history, one that even gets alluded to in literary works by Shakespeare and, later, Dickens.

The British shandy, the German radler, the French picon biere, and even the Mexican michelada are some of the simplest and tastiest examples of low-proof beer cocktails. Look for several examples throughout the book, notably the Dark and Brewy, Passion-Chelada, and the Not-So-Hard Nog Life, as well as several tasty cider sippers.

Possibly the most well-known of the beer cocktails, the shandy is thought to derive from the British slang phrase "shant of gatter" or pub water.

---

8 ounces lager-type beer, chilled

8 ounces lemon or lime soda or ginger ale, chilled

ADD both ingredients to a pint glass and stir gently.

low-proofing your
FAVORITES

Now that you've become familiar with some of the classic low-proof cocktails, why not use the same principals to low-proof your favorite high-ABV cocktails?

Regardless of whether you're a martini man or a margarita señorita, you can easily bring down the ABV of your regular drinks, while still preserving the flavor profiles that made these your faves in the first place. Here's the formula for calculating the proof of your drink:

([Alcohol Content × Liquor Volume] / Total Drink Volume) × 100 = ABV

Now let's remake your modern classics.

The Margarita
Mix It Up: Smoky Stalker

The Reverse Martini
Mix It Up: Lemon Teeny

The Mojito
Mix It Up: Garden Mojo

The Manhattan
Mix It Up: Get Figgy With It

The Bloody Mary
Mix It Up: Garden Mary

The Dark and Stormy
Mix It Up: Dark and Brewy

The Daiquiri
Mix It Up: Mellow Yellow

The Old-Fashioned
Mix It Up: Persimmon Lo-Fashioned

The Mule
Mix It Up: Tokyo Sakura Mule

The Cosmopolitan

THE MARGARITA SERVES 1

A simple sour, the classic margarita is a mix of agave spirit, citrus, and orange liqueur. If you like margaritas, try this low-proof version that uses sherry for the base alcohol, and keeps the tequila (or mezcal, if you like a little smokiness), as the modifier, or seasoning, if you will. You'll never miss the real thing.

1½ ounces Manzanilla sherry
¾ ounce tequila or mezcal
¾ ounce lime juice
¼ ounce Simple Syrup (page 188)
Pinch of salt
Lime wheel

ADD the sherry, tequila, lime juice, syrup, and salt to a mixing glass with ice and shake thoroughly.

STRAIN into a rocks glass filled with fresh ice.

GARNISH with the lime wheel.

bottle spotlight

Once you get comfortable with this basic recipe, feel free to explore other bases for this drink. Lillet Blanc, for instance, is a medium-dry French apéritif made with herbs, spices, and fruits that's fortified with French brandy in a base of Bordeaux wine. It would make an excellent variation that plays up the herbal notes in the tequila. You can find it at most well-stocked liquor stores.

mix it up

SMOKY STALKER `SERVES 1`

Now that you have the basic formula for a low-proof margarita, try this savory variation. The salinity of sherry and the bright, vegetal notes of celery are a synergistic match in Margaritaville.

---

2 celery stalks, washed, trimmed, and cut into 1-inch pieces
1 thin slice serrano pepper, deseeded
¾ ounce lime juice
¾ ounce mezcal or tequila
2 ounces Manzanilla sherry
½ ounce Simple Syrup (page 188)
Black salt

ADD the celery, serrano pepper, and lime juice to a blender and blitz thoroughly.

STRAIN the mixture into a mixing glass with ice and add the mezcal, sherry, syrup, and shake thoroughly.

STRAIN into a rocks glass rimmed with black salt.

bottle spotlight

If you like an extra kick to your drink or don't have peppers on hand, try a spicy tequila such as Ghost Tequila, a 100% agave tequila from Jalisco, Mexico, infused with the infamous ghost peppers from India.

THE MOJITO SERVES 1

Rum, sugar, mint, lime . . . if a refreshing mojito is what you fancy, this lo-fi version swaps high-proof rum for a much lesser proof bittersweet apéritif wine. Less than 1 ounce of traditional white rum is kept for flavor, along with lots of lime and mint.

8 mint leaves

1 ounce aromatized wine such as Cocchi Americano

1 ounce lime juice

¾ ounce silver rum

½ ounce Simple Syrup (page 188)

3 ounces sparkling water

Mint sprigs

ADD the mint leaves to a mixing glass and gently muddle. Add the aromatized wine, lime juice, rum, and syrup to the mixing glass with ice and shake thoroughly.

STRAIN into a highball glass filled with fresh ice and top with the sparkling water.

GARNISH with the mint sprigs.

For fun variations, you can experiment with pineapple or chocolate mint varieties or try replacing the mint with basil, as in the following Garden Mojo recipe.

mix it up

GARDEN MOJO `SERVES 1`

As if the quintessential flavors of a mojito weren't refreshing enough, this riff uses a medley of jasmine tea and honey, muddled with mint and basil, that will send your senses into overdrive.

8 mint leaves

4 basil leaves

1 jasmine tea bag

1 ounce aromatized wine such as Cocchi Americano

1 ounce lime juice

¾ ounce silver rum

½ ounce honey syrup (see Note on page 188)

3 ounces sparkling water

Mint sprigs

Basil sprigs

STEEP the tea for 3 minutes in boiling water. Discard the tea bag and let the tea cool to room temperature.

ADD the mint leaves and basil leaves to the mixing glass and gently muddle. Add the tea, aromatized wine, lime juice, rum, and syrup to the mixing glass with ice and shake thoroughly.

STRAIN into a highball glass filled with fresh ice and top with the sparkling water.

GARNISH with mint and basil sprigs.

bottle spotlight

Cocchi Americano is a crisp Italian aromatized wine, fortified with cinchona bark, citrus, and other botanicals.

THE BLOODY MARY   SERVES 10

Queen of the brunch-tail, the Bloody Mary's spicy and savory combination of tomato juice, horseradish, lemon, and Worcestershire is a true classic that has seen more variations than suitable brunch dates. For this variation, briny amontillado sherry adds low-proof drinkability to a perennial brunch tipple.

8 cups tomato juice
12 ounces Manzanilla sherry
4 ounces vodka or tequila
½ cup lemon juice
4 teaspoons prepared horseradish
1 garlic clove, smashed
Salt and pepper to taste
Celery stalk, lemon wedge, mini garden veggies, etc.

ADD all the ingredients to a blender and blitz thoroughly.

STRAIN into Collins glasses filled with fresh ice.

GARNISH with celery stalk, lemon wedge, mini garden veggies, etc.

mix it up

GARDEN MARY `SERVES 10`

To lend more spicy and earthy unami to your low-proof Mary, try replacing tomatoes with peppers, both mild and hot, for a unique variation.

3 large red peppers, halved and deseeded

12 ounces Manzanilla sherry

4 ounces vodka or tequila

½ cup lemon juice

1 garlic clove, smashed

1 jalapeño, seeded and coarsely chopped

4 teaspoons prepared horseradish

Salt and pepper to taste

Mini garden veggies

PLACE the red peppers on a roasting pan and broil skin side up for 12 to 15 minutes, or until charred. Remove from the oven and set aside to cool. Once cool, use a paring knife to remove the charred skins from the peppers.

ADD the peppers and the rest of the ingredients, except the mini garden veggies, to a blender and blitz thoroughly.

STRAIN into Collins glasses filled with fresh ice.

GARNISH with the mini garden veggies.

bottle spotlight

There's more to sherry than the sweet stuff your grandma kept in her cabinet. There are fino sherries, with dry tart notes; Manzanilla sherries, with briny flavors; and nutty, savory oloroso sherries. All are great for mixing in cocktails.

Garden Mary

Mellow Yellow

THE DAIQUIRI SERVES 1

Only three ingredients (rum, sugar, lime) make up the classic daiquiri, which takes its name from Daquiri, Cuba, the town it was invented in at the turn of the 20th century. To lighten up the proof of this fresh, crisp classic drink, try substituting part of the rum with sweet vermouth bianco.

1 ounce bianco or
    blanc vermouth
1 ounce lime juice
3/4 ounce silver rum
1/2 ounce honey syrup
    (see Note on
    page 188)
Lime wheel

ADD the vermouth, lime juice, rum, and syrup to a mixing glass with ice and shake vigorously.

STRAIN into a chilled coupe or cocktail glass.

GARNISH with the lime wheel.

mix it up

MELLOW YELLOW SERVES 1

This garden-fresh variation pairs sweet yellow peppers with floral chamomile for a fresh, sophisticated sipper.

½ ounce chamomile tea

1 small yellow pepper, halved and deseeded

1 ounce bianco or blanc vermouth

1 ounce lime juice

¾ ounce Havana Club Blanco Rum

½ ounce honey syrup (see Note on page 188)

Lime wedge

Edible flower

STEEP the tea in boiling water for 3 minutes. Remove the tea bag and let the tea cool.

ADD the pepper and the tea to a blender and blitz thoroughly.

STRAIN the mixture into a mixing glass with ice and add the vermouth, lime juice, rum, syrup, and shake vigorously.

STRAIN into a chilled coupe or cocktail glass.

GARNISH with the lime wedge and edible flower.

bottle spotlight

Not to be confused with dry vermouth, bianco or blanc vermouth is the pale, sweet aromatized wine variation, with soft notes of vanilla and florals. Try Martini Bianco for its softer taste.

THE MULE

If you're craving the refreshing ginger beer–based Moscow mule, you'll be delighted with this low-proof shochu variation. Averaging at 30% ABV, Japan's national distilled liquor is just over half as strong as vodka, but it's equally as versatile. There's "oh so mule" you can do!

4 ounces ginger beer
2 ounces shochu
1 ounce lime juice

ADD the ingredients to a mixing glass with ice and stir.

STRAIN into a copper mug filled with crushed ice.

mix it up
TOKYO SAKURA MULE

The sweet, fragrant syrup of sakura blossoms add a soft, intoxicating zing to this low-proof mule. You can mix it directly into the drink or freeze the syrup into ice cubes and let it melt for a subtle burst of flavor.

4 ounces ginger beer
2 ounces shochu
1 ounce lime juice
½ ounce Sakura Syrup
  (page 191)

ADD the ingredients to a mixing glass with ice and stir.

STRAIN into a copper mug filled with crushed ice.

THE REVERSE MARTINI SERVES 1

Take your martini and flip it upside down. By reversing the ratio of gin and vermouth, this martini's elegant flavor stimulates the appetite without knocking you out. It was known to be a favorite of Julia Child.

¾ ounce gin
3¾ ounces dry
   vermouth
Lemon twist

ADD the gin and vermouth to a mixing glass with ice and stir until chilled.

STRAIN into a chilled cocktail glass.

GARNISH with the lemon twist.

mix it up
LEMON TEENY SERVES 1

If you like your martini a little dirty, consider this version where the preserved lemons add a hint of that olive-like umami.

¾ ounce gin
3¾ ounces dry
   vermouth
1 teaspoon preserved
   lemon juice
Lemon twist

ADD the gin, vermouth, and preserved lemon juice to a mixing glass with ice and stir until chilled.

STRAIN into a chilled cocktail glass.

GARNISH with the lemon twist.

For a traditional low-proofed dirty martini, simply swap the preserved lemon juice for the customary olive juice.

THE MANHATTAN SERVES 1

There are other cocktails named for each of New York's boroughs, but none are as popular and timeless as the manhattan. This two-parts whiskey, one-part sweet vermouth, and dash of bitters cocktail of the late 19th century was the first to use vermouth in a drink, even before the martini. To create a much more sessionable drink, equal parts rye and sherry dial down the strength but not the flavor in this classic recipe variation.

¾ ounce sweet vermouth

¾ ounce Amontillado sherry

¾ ounce rye whiskey

2 dashes Angostura bitters

Lemon twist

ADD the vermouth, sherry, rye, and bitters to a mixing glass with ice and stir until chilled.

STRAIN into a chilled coupe.

GARNISH with the lemon twist.

mix it up

GET FIGGY WITH IT SERVES 1

For a fun, flavorful variation, try sweetening up the blend with a spoonful of fig preserves.

¼ ounce sweet vermouth

¾ ounce Amontillado sherry

¾ ounce rye whiskey

½ ounce fig preserves

2 dashes Angostura bitters

Fresh fig slices

ADD the vermouth, sherry, rye, preserves, and bitters to a mixing glass with ice and stir until chilled.

STRAIN into a chilled coupe.

GARNISH with the fig slice.

Get Figgy With It

Dark and Brewy

THE DARK AND STORMY SERVES 1

The simple mix of dark rum and ginger beer that makes up the Dark and Stormy has its roots in colonial Bermuda. As the story has it, officers of the Royal Navy would add a splash of dark, demerara-style rum to their spicy homemade ginger beer. The highball's murky hue was compared to storm clouds, giving it its ominous name. To make this classic low proof, the base of this drink is split between the original rum and a low-ABV amaro.

1 ounce Amaro
    Montenegro
¾ ounce blackstrap
    rum
1 ounce lime juice
4 ounces ginger beer
Lime wedge

ADD the amaro, rum, and lime juice to a Collins glass. Fill with ice and top with the ginger beer.

GARNISH with the lime wedge.

mix it up

DARK AND BREWY `SERVES 1`

To add extra daytime drinkability to this icy, spicy treat, replace the high-proof rum with a lower ABV beer-and-amaro blend.

2 ounces IPA-style
    beer
1 ounce Amaro
    Montenegro
½ ounce Blackstrap
    Molasses Syrup
    (page 188)
1 ounce lime juice
3 ounces ginger beer
Lime wedge

ADD the beer, amaro, syrup, and lime juice to a Collins glass. Fill with ice and top with the ginger beer.

GARNISH with the lime wedge.

bottle spotlight

Amaro Montenegro is made with 40 botanicals in Bologna, Italy. With flavors of orange and caramel, it is bright, bold, and bitter.

THE OLD-FASHIONED SERVES 1

A simple mix of spirit, sugar, and bitters, this bona fide classic is considered the original cocktail. Good versions of the old-fashioned can be found all over the world. For a mindful low-ABV alternative, split the base of whiskey with the much lighter sherry. This blend maintains the punchy, savory notes of the classic.

1 ounce Amontillado sherry
1 ounce rye whiskey
¼ ounce Simple Syrup (page 188)
2 dashes orange bitters
Lemon twist

ADD the sherry, rye, syrup, and bitters to a mixing glass with ice and stir until chilled.

STRAIN into an old-fashioned glass with a fresh ice cube.

GARNISH with the lemon twist.

Persimmon Lo-Fashioned

mix it up

PERSIMMON LO-FASHIONED

SERVES 1

A subtle infusion of flavor from the persimmon and cardamom adds warmth and depth to this flavorful, low-proof variation.

1 ounce Amontillado
   sherry
1 ounce rye whiskey
¼ ounce Persimmon
   Syrup (page 192)
2 dashes cardamom
   bitters
Dehydrated
   persimmon slice

ADD the sherry, rye, syrup, and bitters to a mixing glass with ice and stir until chilled.

STRAIN into an old-fashioned glass with a fresh ice cube.

GARNISH with the persimmon slice.

DRINK WITH BENEFITS

Persimmons are a sweet fruit that reduce inflammation, promote heart health, keep our digestive systems running smoothly, and support good vision. They are chock-full of vitamins, minerals, and fiber.

THE COSMOPOLITAN SERVES 1

Citron vodka, Cointreau, lime juice, and cranberry juice is popularly known as the cosmopolitan, the liquid accessory of the *Sex and the City* gang. Here, it's revamped into a cleaner, lighter accoutrement that will have your girl gang sipping pretty, for far longer.

1½ ounces shochu
1 ounce Cranberry
    Mors (page 215)
¾ ounce orange
    liqueur
¾ ounce lime juice
Orange twist or cherry

ADD the shochu, mors, orange liqueur, and lime juice to a mixing glass with ice and stir until chilled.

STRAIN into a chilled coupe.

GARNISH with the orange twist or a cherry.

bottle spotlight

Shochu is a clean tasting Japanese spirit with less than 25% ABV, distilled from rice, barley, sweet potatoes, or buckwheat.

lo and behold:

FRESH RECIPES

Now that you've been versed in low-proof 101, it's time to have some fun. This next section includes all-new, all-fresh, low-ABV recipes for your long-lasting drinking pleasure.

Eye of the Thai-Ger

Life's a Peach

Bye Bye Birdie

Matcha Colada

La Sirene

Peas & Love

Solmate

Watermelon Frosé

Tipsy Dragon

Culture Club

Mai 24

Ultrasonic

Saffron Apple

Do-Nut Fernet

Lo-Fi Pomerita Punch

First Frost

Boozy Red Velvet

Passion-Chelada

Not-So-Hard Nog Life

Cherry Bombe Soda Float

2-Step Drinks 12 Ways

EYE OF THE THAI-GER SERVES 1

Fiery and refreshing, this sweet and spicy spritz uses crisp sake at its base with a spicy chili vodka as a supporting player. The ginger and lemongrass add traditional Thai flavors to this unique low-proof sipper. It is a drink I can't resist—Thai and stop me.

1½ ounces sake

¾ ounce Tamworth Emshika's Garden Thai Chili Vodka or other high-quality chili vodka

1 stalk lemongrass, cut in two with one-half reserved for garnish

½ ounce Ginger Syrup (page 193)

½ ounce lime juice

6 to 8 cilantro leaves or a pinch of microgreens, plus more for garnish

3 to 4 thin slices Thai chili, plus more for garnish

3 ounces sparkling water

ADD the sake, vodka, lemongrass, syrup, lime juice, cilantro, and chili to a mixing glass with ice and shake until chilled.

STRAIN into a wine goblet filled with fresh ice and top with the sparkling water.

GARNISH with the remaining lemongrass, cilantro leaves, and chili slices.

LIFE'S A PEACH **SERVES 1**

This porch pounder is reminiscent of a classic, front-porch peach tea. This one is big on flavor but mindfully clocks in below the mark, making it easy to come back for another time and again.

¾ ounce bourbon
1½ ounces Pecan-Infused Sherry (page 203)
½ ounce Chai Syrup (page 189)
½ ounce lemon juice
6 fresh peach slices muddled, plus more for garnish
Smoking cinnamon stick (see Note)

ADD the bourbon, sherry, syrup, lemon juice, and peach slices to a mixing glass with ice and shake until chilled.

STRAIN into a chilled coupe or other formal glassware filled with fresh ice.

GARNISH with the peach slices and smoking cinnamon stick.

> *To smoke your cinnamon stick, carefully light the spiced bark, using a long match or lighter. You could also presoak the cinnamon stick in high-proof alcohol to have it burn longer. The flaming stick imparts a beautiful aroma, reminiscent of freshly baked goods.*

BYE BYE BIRDIE SERVES 1

They say birds of a feather flock together, and so do all the ingredients that make up this gorgeously hued, light-as-a-feather sipper. Featuring reverse ratios of gin and vermouth, you won't stop "raven" about it.

1½ ounces dry vermouth

1 ounce cucumber water

¾ ounce gin

½ ounce pineapple

½ ounce lemon juice

½ ounce Butterfly Pea and Lavender Syrup (page 194)

ADD all of the ingredients to a mixing glass with ice and shake until chilled.

STRAIN into a chilled coupe or other fancy glassware.

MATCHA COLADA

If you like piña coladas, you'll love getting caught . . . with this new low-proof variation. It has all the cool, creamy texture of the usual frozen rum, pineapple, and coconut refresher but with an unexpected green tea kick. This colada welcomes a mix of vermouth bianco and lower-proof shochu instead of high-proof rum.

¾ cup pineapple
   chunks
1½ ounces shochu
1 ounce Toasted
   Sesame-Infused
   Bianco Vermouth
   (page 202)
1 ounce coconut milk
½ ounce honey syrup
   (see Note on
   page 188)
1 teaspoon matcha

ADD all of the ingredients to a blender with ice and blitz.

STRAIN into a chilled highball glass or classic hurricane glass.

DRINK WITH BENEFITS

Matcha contains L-theanine, an amino acid that has been shown to reduce stress and promote alertness and focus, can help reduce cell damage and may increase bone mineral density.

LA SIRENE SERVES 1

A tipple worthy of a sea goddess. Without artificial ingredients or colors, drink this beauty as a refreshing nonalcoholic cooler or spike it with a low-proof vermouth.

2 ounces bianco vermouth

1½ ounces pineapple juice

1½ ounces coconut water

½ teaspoon blue spirulina

Sparkling water

ADD the vermouth, pineapple juice, coconut water, and blue spirulina to a mixing glass with ice and stir.

STRAIN into a chilled Nick and Nora glass or coupe and top with the sparkling water.

PEAS & LOVE `SERVES 1`

What the world needs now is love . . . and this fun, botanical spritz with elderflower liqueur and sparkling wine. Built over ice, this elegant spritz welcomes the unexpected freshness of sweet peas. Garnish with a bouquet of aromatic herbs.

1½ ounces St-Germain elderflower liqueur
½ ounce Sweet Pea Syrup (page 195)
½ ounce lemon juice
2 ounces sparkling wine
1 ounce seltzer
Mint leaves
Basil leaves
Watermelon radish slices

ADD the elderflower liqueur, syrup, and lemon juice to a mixing glass with ice and shake thoroughly.

STRAIN into a wine goblet filled with fresh ice and top with the sparkling wine and the seltzer.

GARNISH with the mint, basil, and radish slices.

bottle spotlight

St-Germain was created in 2007 by third generation distiller Robert Cooper. Produced in Beaucaire, in the South of France, St-Germain is infused with fresh elderflowers and filtered with an eau-de-vie wine and neutral spirit.

SOLMATE `SERVES 1`

Bright juicy citrus and spicy turmeric comingle to create a tonic as refreshing as they come. Spiked with dry vermouth, this golden anti-inflammatory elixir tastes just like sunshine should.

2 ounces dry
   vermouth

1 ounce Turmeric
   Switchel (page 212)

1 ounce pineapple
   juice

½ ounce grapefruit
   juice

½ ounce lemon juice

½ ounce honey syrup
   (see Note on
   page 188)

ADD all of the ingredients to a mixing glass with ice and shake thoroughly.

STRAIN into a highball glass filled with fresh ice.

DRINK WITH BENEFITS

Turmeric and its most active compound, curcumin (a natural antioxidant), have very powerful anti-inflammatory benefits that can help improve symptoms of depression and arthritis. Adding black pepper to turmeric increases the bioavailability of curcumin.

WATERMELON FROSÉ

A beautiful twist on everyone's favorite summer treat, this frozen rosé gets sweeter, juicier, and more flavorful with the addition of watermelon and a bitter orange liqueur. Beware of the bitter brain freeze. Bonus: smaller melon halves make the loveliest serving vessels.

1 cup crushed ice

3 ounces Rose Wine (page 206) or dry rosé wine

2 ounces watermelon juice

¼ cup lemon juice

½ ounce bitter orange apéritif (optional)

ADD all of the ingredients to a blender and blitz until smooth.

SERVE in a small watermelon half or glass of your choice.

TIPSY DRAGON SERVES 1

Another hot-weather favorite, these delicious frozen treats can be prepared in advance to make any summer gathering extra special. The berry wine wins you extra points as the tastiest stand-alone pitcher alternative to sangria.

1 cup dragon fruit
½ cup Berry Wine (page 207)
2 tablespoons lemon juice

CUT the dragon fruit into two even halves and use a spoon to remove the flesh.

ADD the dragon fruit flesh and the rest of the ingredients to a blender and blitz until smooth.

POUR the mixture back into the dragon fruit shells or into a sealable freezer-proof container.

FREEZE for 4 to 6 hours, or until frozen. Remove from the freezer and enjoy.

DRINK WITH BENEFITS

Dragon fruit, or pitaya, is a prebiotic—a food that feeds the healthy bacteria in our guts. It specifically encourages the growth of the probiotics lactobacilli and bifidobacteria, which can kill disease-causing viruses and bacteria.

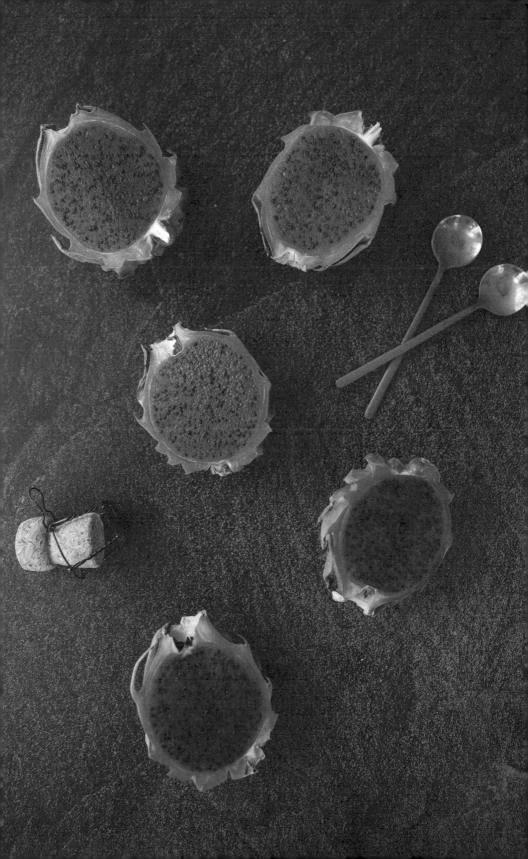

CULTURE CLUB SERVES 1

The creamy tanginess of yogurt adds rich texture and a touch of tartness to this light yet oh-so-smooth adult breakfast tipple. Because we all need a little more culture in our lives.

1 ounce bianco
    vermouth
¾ ounce gin
¾ ounce blueberry
    liqueur
1 tablespoon muddled
    blueberries
1 tablespoon yogurt
½ ounce lemon juice
½ ounce honey

ADD all of the ingredients to a shaker with ice and shake thoroughly.

STRAIN into a highball glass with fresh crushed ice.

DRINK WITH BENEFITS

Yogurt contains probiotics, those friendly bacteria naturally present in our digestive system. These strains of probiotics can help boost the immune system and promote a healthy digestive tract.

MAI 24 `SERVES 1`

Featuring all the island flavors of a mai tai, plus some 24-carrot gold, this enchanting elixir forged with sherry and a splash of rum is likely to put a little extra hop in your step.

1½ ounces Amontillado sherry
1 ounce coconut milk
¾ ounce spiced rum
½ ounce Chai Syrup (page 189)
½ ounce lemon juice
½ ounce carrot juice
½ ounce pineapple juice

ADD all of the ingredients to a mixing glass with ice and shake until chilled.

STRAIN into a chilled coupe or a highball glass filled with fresh pebble or crushed ice.

ULTRASONIC SERVES 1

A fruit-forward, dry white wine is unsurpassable on a hot summer day. Unsurpassed, that is, unless it's transformed into a delicious spritzer with these effortless and irresistible touches. Beware: You may never enjoy a plain white wine again.

3 Kiwi Ice Cubes (page 201)

3 ounces aromatic white wine, such as Riesling or sauvignon blanc

1 ounce club soda

1 dash yuzu or grapefruit bitters

PUT the kiwi ice cubes in a wine glass and add the wine.

TOP off with the club soda and bitters.

SAFFRON APPLE SERVES 1

Our favorite childhood snow cone is all grown up in this elegant boozy expression, built on hard cider, floral liqueur, and cognac. Shaved ice never tasted this good.

3 ounces hard apple cider

1½ ounces Italicus

¾ ounce cognac

¾ ounce Saffron Rose Syrup (page 195)

Rose petals

Saffron threads

ADD the cider, Italicus, cognac, and syrup to a mixing glass with ice and shake thoroughly.

STRAIN into a glass filled with fresh shaved ice.

GARNISH with the rose petals and saffron threads.

DRINK WITH BENEFITS

Saffron can enhance libido, boost mood, and improve memory. Saffron also appears to help treat PMS symptoms, such as irritability, pain, and anxiety. It may have aphrodisiac properties for both men and women.

DO-NUT FERNET SERVES 1

Known as "the bartender's handshake," Fernet-Branca is a popular shot of choice among bartender industry insiders. Often an acquired taste, this distinctly bitter liqueur pairs incredibly well with coffee in this low-proof cold brew cocktail served with a special sweet treat. You're not likely to "fernet" this dessert sipper.

---

2 ounces Fernet-Branca

2 ounces coconut cream

2 ounces cold brew coffee

Donut with Fernet Glaze (page 211)

ADD the Fernet-Branca, coconut cream, and coffee to a mixing glass with ice and shake thoroughly.

STRAIN into a highball glass filled with fresh ice.

GARNISH with the Fernet-glazed donut.

bottle spotlight

Fernet-Branca is an Italian amaro that's made with myrrh, rhubarb, chamomile, cardamom, aloe, and saffron, among other herbs and spices, and has a base of grape-distilled spirits.

LO-FI POMERITA PUNCH SERVES 10

With the ease of a big-batch cocktail, this pretty
pomegranate margarita punch won't knock you out.
This pitcher-perfect drink is fortified with sherry and is
seasoned with a spicy tequila or mezcal for a touch of
familiar smokiness without the high-proof kick.

½ cup honey syrup
(see Note on
page 188)
½ cup lemon juice
2 cups Olorosso
sherry
1 cup Ghost Tequila or
mezcal
1 cup pomegranate
juice
Pomegranate arils
Citrus slices

ADD the honey syrup and lemon juice to a
bowl and mix thoroughly. Pour into an ice-
filled punch bowl and add the sherry, tequila,
and pomegranate juice.

GARNISH individual servings with the fresh
pomegranate arils and the citrus slices.

DRINK WITH BENEFITS

Pomegranates contain more than 100 phytochemicals; are a good
source of fiber as well as vitamins A, C, some B vitamins; and contain
minerals such as calcium, potassium, and iron. Pomegranate juice also is
rich in antioxidant polyphenols—powerful antioxidants that help remove
free radicals, protect cells from damage, and reduce inflammation.

FIRST FROST SERVES 1

The classic three-equal-part Italian negroni might be the perfect drink. But for a lower-octane variation, this low-proof riff on a white negroni is just the ticket. Maintaining the balance with flowery Lillet and bitter Suze, but replacing the high-proof gin with a decidedly lower-ABV shochu, this version gets a frosty winter makeover with a touch of blue spirulina.

1½ ounces shochu
1 ounce Spruce-
    Infused Lillet Blanc
    (page 204)
¾ ounce Suze
½ teaspoon blue
    spirulina

ADD all the ingredients to a mixing glass with ice and stir until chilled.

STRAIN into your desired vessel.

DRINK WITH BENEFITS
Spirulina is one of the most nutrient-dense foods, featuring high concentrations of nutrients, including protein, iron, potassium, zinc, calcium, and B vitamins. Spirulina is also a powerful detoxifier that assists the body in flushing out toxins, including heavy metals.

BOOZY RED VELVET

SERVES 1

This festive red velvet hot chocolate gets a low-ABV upgrade that's guaranteed to fortify against the winter chill. Enjoy this tasty jeweled sipper warm or over ice.

½ cup Oat Milk (page 211) or milk of choice

¼ cup beet juice

½ ounce Saffron Rose Syrup (page 195)

1 teaspoon cacao powder

1½ ounces bitter liqueur

ADD the oat milk, beet juice, syrup, and cacao powder to a saucepan and stir until smooth and creamy. Simmer over low heat for 2 to 3 minutes. Remove from the heat.

POUR into a mug and add the liqueur.

DRINK WITH BENEFITS

Beet juice offers a concentrated dose of antioxidants, nitrates, vitamins, and minerals. Beets also contain phytonutrients that fight inflammation and facilitate the detoxification of the liver and kidneys.

PASSION-CHELADA `SERVES 1`

The classic michelada—the south of the border hangover cure consisting of beer, salt, lime, spice, and juice—has a way of kicking up the flavor of a nice, cold beer. This low-voltage drink gets a tropical makeover with the flavors of passion fruit and habanero.

1 slice habanero, deseeded
1 ounce passion fruit puree
1 cup Mexican lager
Hibiscus Salt for rim (page 210)

ADD the habanero to a mixing glass and muddle gently. Add the passion fruit puree and lager to the mixing glass with ice and shake thoroughly.

STRAIN into a tall glass filled with fresh ice and rimmed with Hibiscus Salt.

NOT-SO-HARD NOG LIFE `SERVES 1`

One of the more popular recipes in my first cocktail book, *Zen and Tonic*, was for a vegan eggnog recipe that I coined the Hard Nog Life. It seemed only appropriate to share a low-proof variation with you here, using a creamy stout, coconut cream, and a chai syrup. The result is a truly synergistic holiday blend.

¾ ounce Chai Syrup (page 189)

2 ounces coconut cream, plus more for garnish

4 ounces stout-style beer

Pinch of grated nutmeg

Pinch of grated cinnamon

ADD the syrup and the coconut cream to a tall glass and mix well. Top with the beer and stir again.

GARNISH with extra coconut cream and dash each of nutmeg and cinnamon.

CHERRY BOMBE SODA FLOAT

SERVES 1

Cherry vanilla ice cream float meets summertime spritz. This sweet and celebratory boozy dessert is an ode to my favorite women and food community, Cherry Bombe, for encouraging endless creativity in the kitchen.

1½ ounces St. Agrestis Inferno Bitter red apéritif
¾ ounce Ginger Syrup (page 193)
1 scoop cherry vanilla ice cream
3 ounces sparkling wine

ADD the apéritif and syrup to a cocktail shaker with ice and shake.

STRAIN the mixture into a highball or soda float glass filled with the ice cream, and top with sparkling wine.

BREAK THE ICE: MAKER'S SPOTLIGHT

Based in Brooklyn, New York, brothers Louie and Matt Catizone, along with long-time friend and industry veteran Steven DeAngelo, wanted to create a product made with real herbs, spices, and citrus that honored the old-world methods of Italy, where their dad was born. With real attention to detail, perfect extractions, and individual macerations for different lengths of time, the pressed, blended, and aged St. Agrestis's red bitter aperitivo and amaro both really stand out. Made for real aperitivo and digestivo drinkers.

2-STEP DRINKS 12 WAYS   SERVES 1

Want a delicious low-octane drink without the fuss? Try these 12 delicious flavor combos that you can build directly in your glass. Just keep lots of citrus on hand for a fresh squeeze.

Suze + tonic

St. George Spirits Bruto Americano + botanical tonic

Shochu + yuzu tonic

Lillet Rose + ginger kombucha

Bonolo Amaro + cold brew

Martini Bianco + sparkling coconut water

Sweet vermouth + bitter lemon soda

Italicus + grapefruit soda

White port + elderflower tonic

St. Agrestis apéritif + pineapple juice

St-Germain Elderflower Liqueur + soda

Pineau des Charentes + bitter lemon soda

bottle spotlight

Pineau des Charentes is a French apéritif made with slightly fermented grape must and cognac. For a comprehensive list of suggested bottles, head to Low-ABV Bottles to Know on page 217.

DRINKS WITH BENEFITS
Originally used as a preventative against malaria, tonic water is a bitter-sweet carbonated drink made with quinine. It's most famous pairing is with gin, but crisp and refreshing tonic in its many varieties will also highlight many of the low-proof bottles listed above.

big batch,
LOW-PROOFED

Throwing a party? Don't get stuck playing bartender all night. The following low-ABV sippers make the perfect party punches. These four foolproof batched recipes keep it big on taste and low on stress, so you can keep the party going a little longer with the rest of your guests.

Tropic Like It's Hot

Aloe Can You Go

Jet Set Reset

Amore for Amaro

TROPIC LIKE IT'S HOT SERVES 10

This tropical twist on the spritz features a touch of spice that will turn up the heat on any party.

2 cups Suze
1 cup pineapple juice
1 cup passion fruit
    puree
1 red chili pepper,
    minced
1 cup sparkling wine
½ cup sparkling water

ADD the Suze, pineapple juice, passion fruit puree, and pepper to a punch bowl or pitcher.

ADD ice, the sparkling wine, and the sparkling water just before serving.

ALOE CAN YOU GO

Delicate and floral, this soothing and cooling sparkler keeps you hydrated and refreshed.

---

2 cups St-Germain
   Elderflower Liqueur
1 cup aloe water
1 cup coconut water
½ cup Butterfly Pea
   and Lavender Syrup
   (page 194)
½ cup lemon juice
2 cups sparkling wine

ADD the St-Germain, aloe water, coconut water, syrup, and lemon juice to a punch bowl or pitcher.

ADD ice and the sparkling wine just before serving.

JET SET RESET SERVES 10 TO 12

Incorporate some detox into your retox with this fresh, herbal punch with green tea and honeydew.

3 cups dry vermouth

2 cups green tea

½ cup Yellow Chartreuse

½ cup Honeydew Syrup (page 196)

½ cup lime juice

¼ cup mint leaves

¼ cup basil leaves

1 serrano pepper, thinly sliced

4 kiwis, sliced

ADD the vermouth, tea, Chartreuse, syrup, and lime juice to a punch bowl or pitcher with ice.

GARNISH with the mint, basil, peppers, and kiwi.

bottle spotlight

The main differences between Green and Yellow Chartreuse are the color, the proof, and the sweetness. Green Chartreuse is the more complex of the two, clocking in at 55% ABV, with a natural green color and heavy herbal taste. Yellow Chartreuse, at 40% ABV, is milder and sweeter with botanicals such as saffron and honey contributing to its natural yellow color. Try them both—and remember that a little goes a long way!

AMORE FOR AMARO SERVES 12

With a bright citrus and aromatic herbal profile, the bittersweet amaro is brightened up with crisp dry cider and sparkling ginger beer to create a perfect low-proof punch.

2 cups Amaro
    Montenegro
2 cups apple cider
2 cups ginger beer or
    ginger kombucha
Apple slices

ADD the Montenegro and cider to a punch bowl or pitcher.

ADD ice and the ginger beer just before serving. Garnish with the apple slices.

guest recipes + MAKER'S SPOTLIGHTS

With low-ABV cocktails as popular as ever, I was pushed to share some of the unique low-proof drinks being offered in bars across the nation. I'm continually inspired by the creativity of the new generations of makers and shakers, and I'm excited to feature recipes from notable drink creators who have their own takes on the low-proof cocktail. I hope these recipes inspire you as much as they have delighted me.

GODZILLA `SERVES 1`

Jillian Vose, the bar manager and beverage director of the award-winning Dead Rabbit NYC, is behind many of the bar's most inventive cocktails. Here, she shares her recipe for this delicious sparkler.

---

1 dash Peychaud's
  bitters
1 teaspoon cinnamon
  bark syrup (see
  Note on page 193)
1 ounce Lillet Rose
½ ounce Clear Creek
  Eau de Vie de
  Pomme 8 year
1½ ounce Italicus
1 ounce champagne
1 ounce sparkling water

ADD the bitters, syrup, Lillet Rose, eau de vie, and Italicus to a mixing glass with crushed ice. Whip shake (see Note) until the ice dissolves.

STRAIN into a highball glass with hand-cracked ice and top with the champagne and sparkling water.

bottle spotlight

Italicus, known in the mid-19th century as the "drink of kings," is made with a base of Italian bergamot and other Italian botanicals, including rose petals.

A shaking technique often used when making a fluffy mai tai or a frothy Ramos gin fizz, the whip shake consists of mixing cocktails with only a few pieces of crushed ice or one larger ice cube. Shaking with less ice allows for more of a whipping of the ingredients, and chills the drink without overdiluting it—especially vital when pouring over quick-melting crushed or pebbled ice.

CAN'T ELOPE

SERVES 1

It's hard to beat the bright, floral flavor of melons. Bartender Lily Jenson of the Miami Soho Beach House preserves this melon goodness in a syrup, which can be used all year round, and imparts it in her smoky and floral sparkler.

¾ ounce Joven Ilegal Mezcal

¾ ounce St-Germain Elderflower Liqueur

½ ounce Martini & Rossi Bianco Vermouth

1 ounce cantaloupe syrup (see Note on page 196)

Sparkling wine

Cantaloupe slice

COMBINE the mezcal, liqueur, vermouth, and syrup in a cocktail shaker with ice. Shake vigorously until chilled. Double strain into a wine glass with ice. Garnish with the slice of cantaloupe.

SHOCHU 50/50 `SERVES 1`

Los Angeles–based bartender Jason Yu loves using shochu in his low-proof drinks. The spirit generally falls between the 20% to 30% ABV category, but "what it tones down in naughty juice, it more than makes up for in character, body, and flavor," says Yu.

1½ ounces Nankai shochu

1½ ounces Dolin dry vermouth

2 dashes Scrappy's bergamot bitters

Pickled lotus root slice

ADD the shochu and vermouth to a mixing glass with ice and stir.

STRAIN into a Nick and Nora glass and add the bitters.

GARNISH with the lotus root slice.

bottle spotlight

Shochu is a traditional Japanese distilled spirit typically made from barley, sweet potato, or in the case of Nankai, sugarcane and rice. Shochu uses koji, the same fermentation starter as miso or soy sauce, making it unique from other spirits like whiskey or vodka. Genuine shochu is also single-distilled, retaining the flavors and aromas of the ingredients. Nankai has a clean, smooth flavor that enhances savory/umami, salt, bitter, and sour flavors.

SHIFT BREAK SERVES 1

At the Sparrow Rooftop in Fort Lauderdale, Florida, the newest bar from the award-winning team of Death & Co., Eric Vincent breaks for a smooth tipple, seasoned with Irish whiskey and a lovely pear brandy.

1½ ounces Del Professore dry vermouth

¾ ounce Teeling Small-Batch Irish Whiskey

¼ ounce St. George Spirits Pear Brandy

2 drops Absinthe Bitters (page 208)

Grated nutmeg

ADD the vermouth, whiskey, and brandy in a mixing glass with ice and stir to dilution.

STRAIN into a chilled coupe.

GARNISH with the bitters and the grated nutmeg.

bottle spotlight

Founded in 1982 by Jorg Rupf, a pioneer in what has become the craft distilling movement, St. George Spirits started out as an eau de vie distillery. They have steadily expanded their portfolio to include over a dozen spirits as well as their Raspberry Liqueur, Spiced Pear Liqueur, NOLA Coffee Liqueur, and Bruto Americano—an American-style aperitivo with flavor that evokes Maine's balsam fir and California buckthorn bark.

SANTA ROSA `SERVES 1`

Cocktail chef Matthew Biancaniello, who's known for creating adventurous culinary-inspired libations, shares a drink using verjus—a tart juice made by pressing unripe grapes—in this inventive nonalcoholic sipper. If you've never had candy cap mushrooms, you're in for a treat. This flavorful mushroom has a faint scent of maple syrup, burnt sugar, and even notes of curry.

¾ ounce lime juice
¾ ounce agave syrup
    (see Note on
    page 188)
2 Santa Rosa plums,
    halved and pitted
Pinch of huacatay
2 ounces Candy Cap
    Mushroom Verjus
    Infusion (page 205)
Marigold petals

ADD the lime juice, syrup, plums, and huacatay to a mixing glass and muddle. Add the infusion and ice and shake thoroughly.

STRAIN into a rocks glass filled with fresh ice.

GARNISH with the marigold petals.

bottle spotlight

Verjus is the pressed juice of unripened grapes. It can be red, made from red grapes; it can be white, made from white grapes; or it can be a red-white mix. Verjus has a sweet-tart taste with a milder flavor than vinegar. Unlike wine, verjus is not fermented and is not alcoholic. You can find verjus from specialty grocers or online.

SIZZLE REEL SANGAREE SERVES 1

The robust caramel flavors and nutty aromas of Taylor Fladgate 10 Year Old Tawny Port are livened and brightened with a splash of gin and Chartreuse in this aromatic creation by Lukas B. Smith, creative director and partner at Cotton & Reed, the first rum distillery in Washington, DC.

2 ounces Taylor Fladgate 10 Year Old Tawny Port (see Note)
½ ounce Spring44 gin
¼ ounce Green Chartreuse
¼ ounce lemon juice
1 dash Bitter Truth Jerry Thomas' Own Decanter Bitters
Lemon wheel
Lemon twist or dehydrated lemon wheel

ADD the port, gin, Chartreuse, juice, and bitters to a mixing glass. Drop in the lemon wheel just before adding ice and shake until chilled.

STRAIN into a chilled Nick and Nora glass or small coupe glass.

ADD the bitters and garnish with the lemon twist or dehydrated wheel.

Lukas notes that the tawny port could be substituted for a ruby port if serving many guests.

bottle spotlight

Green Chartreuse is a naturally green liqueur made from 130 herbs and other plants macerated in alcohol. The liqueur has been made by the Carthusian monks since 1737.

THE STOLEN MOON SERVES 1

The warm flavors of chai tea comingle with the sweet amaro and nutty orgeat in a delightful way in Alyssa Sartor's rum cocktail. Alyssa and her partner, longtime Death & Co. manager Frankie Rodriguez, spotlight classic Italian spirits in imaginative ways at August Laura, their Italian cocktail bar in the Carroll Gardens neighborhood of Brooklyn, New York.

1 ounce Chai-Infused Stolen Rum (page 204)
1 ounce Bràulio amaro
¾ ounce Orgeat (page 199)
¾ ounce lime juice
Mint sprig
Grated nutmeg

COMBINE all the ingredients except the mint sprig and grated nutmeg in a cocktail shaker with ice, lightly shake, and strain into a mug. Top with pebble ice. Garnish with mint sprig and nutmeg shaved over the ice and sprig.

bottle spotlight

Stolen Smoked Rum is a one-of-a-kind rum distilled in Trinidad from sugar cane and aged in whiskey barrels for up to 2 years. It's then infused with smoked American hardwood and Moroccan fenugreek as well as Arabica Colombian coffee and Madagascan vanilla.

GREEN LIGHT `SERVES 1`

Bright, refreshing sippers are always delightful, but this one from Italian bartender Giorgia Crea has an alluring complexity from the addition of oleo saccharum. Oleo saccharum, which means "oily sugar" in Latin, is made using a classic technique where citrus peels are macerated with sugar to create a deliciously complex mixture that's often used in punch recipes.

1 celery stalk

½ small cucumber

1 ounce Gra'it Grappa

¾ ounce Oleo Saccharum–Infused Lemon Juice (page 198)

1½ ounces East Imperial Yuzu Tonic

Lemon twist

JUICE or blend the celery and the cucumber and strain out the pulp. Add 1 ounce of the celery-cucumber juice to a white wine glass.

ADD the grappa, juice, and tonic to the glass. Fill with ice and stir gently.

GARNISH with the lemon twist..

BREAK THE ICE: MAKER'S SPOTLIGHT

Gra'it Grappa, an Italian grape-based pomace brandy from Italy's renowned Veneto region, is produced by a fourth-generation distillery that stands out due to its commitment to the environment. Their sustainability efforts include the collection and storage of raw materials to preserve aromatic integrity, flexible distillation, aging, and packaging and by-product enhancements. Their state-of-the-art distillery also adopts sustainable and renewable energy technology that enables it to generate 85% of the energy it uses annually from their distillation. They also make a grappa-based amaro that's infused with notes of dried stone fruits, chocolate, nuts, and spicy rye and maple.

ALL NIGHT LONG

SERVES 1

At Repour Bar in Miami Beach, Florida, folks enjoy this refreshing sipper "all night long," courtesy of bar manager Peter Siewruk. And now, you too can have a little taste of Miami Beach right at home. This beautiful photo was taken for Repour Bar by 52Chefs' photographer Anthony Nader.

2 ounces Lillet Blanc

1 ounce cucumber juice

½ ounce strawberry juice

¼ ounce lemon juice

Ginger beer

Strawberry slices

Mint sprigs

Edible flowers

ADD the Lillet, cucumber juice, strawberry juice, and lemon juice to a mixing glass with ice and shake thoroughly.

STRAIN into a wine glass filled with fresh ice and top with ginger beer.

GARNISH with the strawberries, mint, and edible flowers.

bottle spotlight

The first martini James Bond ordered in Ian Fleming's 1953 book, *Casino Royale*, was the Vesper martini: "Three measures of Gordon's, one of vodka, half a measure of Kina Lillet. Shake it very well until it's ice-cold, then add a large thin slice of lemon-peel. Got it?" Kina Lillet, now simply called Lillet, is a French apéritif made from a blend of wine, liqueurs, fruits, and herbs.

BORROWING FROM OTHERS IN TIME `SERVES 1`

Known as the Cocktail Whisperer, Warren Bobrow is a freelance mixologist and six-time author specializing in craft spirits and cannabis cocktails. Here, he creates a fun little THC/CBD refresher that has its roots in early apothecary.

½ ounce Lucid Absinthe or other high-quality absinthe

6 ounces mint-infused lemonade

2 dashes Peychaud's bitters

4 to 5 drops tincture of ½ THC to ½ CBD on a glycerin base

Pinch of sea salt

ADD the absinthe to a chilled Collins glass. Fill with crushed ice and top with the mint lemonade. Add more crushed ice and dash the bitters on top.

DRIP the THC-CBD tincture over the bitters (10 mg at most).

GARNISH with the sea salt and a nonplastic straw.

DRINKS WITH BENEFITS

This is a very low-ABV drink, and it features just a touch of THC to create the "entourage effect." The entourage effect is achieved when CBD is used in combination with THC to maximize the therapeutic effects of both compounds.

OAXACA GRACE

SERVES 1

This refreshing sipper—from Matthew Rose of Monzú, a Sicilian eatery in Las Vegas, Nevada—brings out the best in all its ingredients. Mezcal and watermelon are a pair made in heaven, brightened up further by the Ramazzotti aperitivo and hint of heat from the chili bitters.

4 to 5 cubes watermelon

¾ ounce Mezcal Veras Joven

1½ ounces Ramazzotti Amaro

¾ ounce lemon juice

¾ ounce Simple Syrup (page 188)

2 dashes smoked chili bitters

Soda water

Watermelon slice, dusted with Tajín

ADD the watermelon cubes to a mixing glass and muddle. Add the mezcal, Ramazzotti, lemon juice, syrup, and ice and shake thoroughly.

STRAIN into a wine glass filled with fresh ice and add the bitters.

GARNISH with the watermelon slice.

bottle spotlight

Ramazzotti is a delightfully floral and fresh aperitivo from the region of Ramazzotti in Italy, which has been producing bitter amaro since 1815. Their Aperitivo Rosato has seductive notes of hibiscus and orange blossoms alongside hints of basil.

HOLLYWOOD TO HOUSTON `SERVES 1`

This "tailor-made" buck cocktail created by Charlie Shapiro from the one-of-a-kind drinkery and custom tailor shop—Char Bar, in the Market Square Park area of downtown Houston—combines bourbon and peach in a classic pairing with a low-proof twist.

1 ounce Duke Bourbon
½ ounce Mathilde Pêche liqueur
½ ounce lemon juice
2 ounces Fever-Tree Ginger Beer
Fresh peach slices

ADD the bourbon, liqueur, and lemon juice to a mixing glass or copper mug with ice and shake until chilled.

STRAIN into a Collins glass or copper mug filled with fresh ice and top with the ginger beer.

GARNISH with the peach slices.

BREAKFAST IN TOKYO SERVES 1

A favorite of Pomp & Whimsy founder Dr. Nicola Nice, this easy sipper brightens up any morning. A trip to Japan is optional.

1 ounce Pomp &
   Whimsy Gin
   Liqueur
1 ounce nigori sake
1 ounce cucumber
   juice
Cucumber slice
Edible flower

ADD the liqueur, sake, and cucumber juice to a mixing glass with ice and shake until chilled.

STRAIN into an old-fashioned glass filled with fresh ice.

GARNISH with the cucumber slice and edible flower.

BREAK THE ICE: MAKER'S SPOTLIGHT

Founded by Dr. Nicola Nice, a trained sociologist, self-confessed cocktail obsessive, and advisor to some of world's top spirits companies, Pomp & Whimsy is a cordial-style gin inspired by the female culinary writers and home brewers of the Victorian era. Made from scratch in Los Angeles using a select blend of 16 natural and whole ingredients, Pomp & Whimsy is a highly refined yet playfully sensorial spirit that can be enjoyed by itself or in a number of reimagined cocktails.

GUANALOPE `SERVES 1`

Dustin Bolin is the beverage director at Tuck Shop Kitchen & Bar in the heart of the Coronado Historic District in Phoenix, Arizona. He created this dry-yet-sweet melon cocktail with a bitter finish.

3 to 4 basil leaves, plus more for garnish
1-inch strip lemon peel
1 ounce Fortaleza Blanco Tequila
½ ounce Bittermans Citron Sauvage liqueur
¼ ounce Spanish dry vermouth
¾ ounce Cantaloupe Shrub (page 213)

ADD the basil leaves and lemon peel to a mixing glass and muddle. Add the tequila, liqueur, vermouth, shrub, and ice and stir.

STRAIN into a chilled coupe glass.

GARNISH with a basil leaf.

DRINKS WITH BENEFITS
Shrubs, also known as drinking vinegars, have a long history as health tonics. It is said that Hippocrates prescribed a tonic of apple cider vinegar and honeycomb to cure colds. In Asia, fruit- or honey-infused vinegar was consumed after meals to help digestion. Other benefits include stabilizing blood sugars, lowering cholesterol, and maintaining alkaline pH balance.

JUANITO AMOR SERVES 1

This simple, crowd-pleasing tiki tipple has all the flavor of a high-proof drink in a friendly ABV format. The recipe comes from Cassidy Moser of Kreepy Tiki fame. Moser now creates tiki magic at Jewel of the South in New Orleans, Louisiana.

2 ounces Amontillado sherry
1½ ounces pineapple juice
½ ounce Orgeat (page 199)
½ ounce lemon juice
Mint sprig
Edible flower

ADD the sherry, pineapple juice, syrup, and lemon juice to the mixing glass with ice and shake thoroughly.

STRAIN into a tall glass filled with fresh ice.

GARNISH with the mint sprig and edible flower.

SANGRITO `SERVES 1`

I first met Keith Popejoy while he was bar manager and head bartender at the acclaimed bar Death or Glory, in Delray Beach, Florida. I often wondered about his low-proof shift drink while I sipped on my negroni. Wonder no more—here it is, in all its delicious glory.

2 ounces sauvignon
    blanc
¾ ounce Mint
    Demerara Syrup
    (page 197)
¾ ounce lime juice
½ ounce grapefruit
    liqueur
8 to 10 mint leaves
Club soda
Lime wheel
Mint sprig

ADD the wine, syrup, lime juice, grapefruit liqueur, and mint leaves to a mixing glass with ice and shake thoroughly.

STRAIN into a snifter filled with crushed ice and top with club soda.

GARNISH with the lime wheel and mint sprig..

DUBONNET SPRITZ

Queen Elizabeth II sips on gin and Dubonnet, but Walter Johnson, head bartender of the prestigious Bath and Tennis Club in Palm Beach, Florida, prefers this refreshing Dubonnet spritz instead.

3 ounces prosecco

1½ ounces Dubonnet

1 ounce sparkling water

Orange slice

FILL a wine glass with ice and add the processo, Dubonnet, and sparkling water.

GARNISH with the orange slice.

FAR EASTSIDE

SERVES 1

At the rooftop lounge of the Ravel Hotel in Long Island City, New York, Asian fusion fare is paired with several sake cocktails. Among these libations, the unique, low-ABV Far Eastside combines the fresh crispness of gin and cucumber juice with the unique spice of wasabi.

1½ ounces Hiro sake

¾ ounce gin

1 ounce cucumber juice

¼ teaspoon wasabi

½ ounce lemon juice

½ ounce Simple Syrup (page 188)

8 mint leaves

Cucumber ribbons

ADD the sake, gin, cucumber juice, wasabi, lemon juice, syrup, and mint leaves to a mixing glass with ice and shake thoroughly.

STRAIN into a chilled coupe.

GARNISH with the cucumber ribbons.

BREAK THE ICE: MAKER'S SPOTLIGHT

Hiro is a handcrafted sake from the Taiyo Shuzo Brewery in Japan's famed Niigata prefecture. Hiro sake is an homage to the ancient beverages of samurai Hiroemon Takeda, who mastered the art of brewing sake nearly 200 years ago. Two sake offerings from this artisanal producer are made for the modern drinking experience: Hiro Red, a Junmai-style sake, presents a clean and subtle earthy character with a finish that hints of apple. Hiro Blue, a Junmai Ginjo-style sake, is made by polishing away the outer layers of the rice grains until only small "pearls" remain.

PACIFIC CREST TRAIL `SERVES 1`

At her bar Hello Stranger in Oakland, California, Summer-Jane Bell loves adding savory notes to cocktails with fresh herbs, like the following sipper with orange and thyme. The vermouth and sherry add roundness and depth, while the blood orange liqueur adds a pop of bright citrus flavor in this low-proof spritzer.

6 sprigs of thyme, plus more for garnish
¾ ounce Pür·Likör Spice Blood Orange Liqueur
1 ounce Vya Whisper vermouth (or your favorite dry vermouth)
¾ ounce Manzanilla sherry
½ ounce lemon juice
Soda water

ADD the thyme to a mixing glass and gently muddle. Add the liqueur, vermouth, sherry, lemon juice, and ice and shake thoroughly.

STRAIN into a wine glass and top with soda water.

GARNISH with a thyme sprig.

BREAK THE ICE: MAKER'S SPOTLIGHT

One of only a handful of female distillers and spirit brand owners, Kiki Braverman, combines her interests in fermentation, brewing, biodynamic methods of farming, and craftsmanship to bring us her brand, Pür·Spirits. With a very contemporary view on fresh, local, and organic ingredients, Pür·Spirits makes pear, elderflower, and blood orange liqueurs; a sloe gin; and an apéritif-style amaro.

CAPRESE COOLER

In a uniquely low-waste approach to low-proof, Will Benedetto of New York City's restaurant Woodpecker reimagines what the kitchen might consider waste into delicious cocktail ingredients. Using the restaurant's own caprese salad as inspiration, Will uses sweet basil, mozzarella, and melon in a low-ABV highball.

1 ounce Spring44 vodka
¼ ounce fruit vinegar
1 ounce mozzarella brine
1 ounce Tomato Basil Water (page 214)
3 drops Black Pepper Tincture (page 205)
3 rock melon balls, skewered
Balsamic vinegar

ADD the vodka, fruit vinegar, mozzarella brine, water, and tincture to a mixing glass with ice and shake vigorously.

STRAIN into a highball glass filled with fresh ice.

GARNISH with the melon balls and drizzle with the balsamic vinegar.

This drink is meant to be a study in sustainability, and Will encourages us to use the pulpy remainder of the tincture as a base for soups or red sauce.

supporting RECIPES

Simple Syrup

Blackstrap Molasses Syrup

Chai Syrup

Hibiscus & Pink Peppercorn Syrup

Date Syrup

Sakura Syrup

Persimmon Syrup

Ginger Syrup

Butterfly Pea and Lavender Syrup

Sweet Pea Syrup

Saffron Rose Syrup

Honeydew Syrup

Mint Demerara Syrup

Oleo Saccharum–Infused
Lemon Juice

Orgeat

Edible Flower Ice Cubes

Cherry and Bitter Orange Liqueur
Kiwi ice Cubes

Raspberry, Rose, and Chocolate
Bianco Vermouth

Toasted Sesame-Infused
Bianco Vermouth

Pecan-Infused Sherry

Spruce-Infused Lillet Blanc

Chai-Infused Stolen Rum

Candy Cap Mushroom
Verjus Infusion

Black Pepper Tincture

Rose Wine

Berry Wine

Absinthe Bitters

Five-Spice Bitters

Chocolate Chili Bitters

Herbes de Provence Salt

Hibiscus Salt

Cardamom Sugar Fernet Glaze

Oat Milk

Turmeric Switchel

Cantaloupe Shrub

Tomato Basil Water

Cranberry Mors

SIMPLE SYRUP `MAKES 1 CUP`

This is the classic way to add sweetness to your cocktails.

1 cup granulated sugar
1 cup water

ADD the sugar and water to a saucepan and bring to a simmer over medium heat. Simmer, stirring occasionally, until the sugar has dissolved. Remove from the heat and let cool.

TRANSFER to a glass jar and store in the refrigerator for up to 1 month.

You can substitute raw honey, maple syrup, coconut sugar, agave nectar, or any of the refined sugar alternatives listed on page 34 for the granulated sugar.

BLACKSTRAP MOLASSES SYRUP `MAKES 1 CUP`

An excellent source of minerals, blackstrap molasses pairs well with dark spirits and fall and winter fruits.

1 cup blackstrap molasses
1 cup water

ADD the molasses and water to a saucepan and bring to a simmer over medium heat. Simmer, stirring occasionally, until the molasses has dissolved. Remove from the heat and let cool.

TRANSFER to a glass jar and store in the refrigerator for up to 1 month.

CHAI SYRUP `MAKES 2 CUPS`

This aromatic sweetener turns chai tea into a delicious syrup that you can use on anything from ice cream to pancakes. Of course, you can also use this simple syrup in several cocktails featured in this book.

8 green cardamom
   pods
½ teaspoon black
   peppercorns
½ teaspoon whole
   cloves
2 tablespoons fresh
   ginger, chopped
1 cup coconut sugar
1 cup water

CRUSH the cardamom pods and black peppercorns. Place the cardamom, peppercorns, and cloves in a frying pan and toast over low heat until very aromatic, about 5 minutes (optional).

ADD the toasted spices, ginger, sugar, and water to a saucepan and bring to a simmer over medium heat. Simmer, stirring often, for 5 to 10 minutes. Remove from the heat and let cool.

STRAIN the syrup into a glass jar and store in the refrigerator for up to 1 month.

HIBISCUS & PINK PEPPERCORN SYRUP `MAKES 2 CUPS`

This duo of mildly spicy pink peppercorns and tart, magenta-hued hibiscus conspires to add a delightful kick to both low- and nonalcoholic offerings.

1 cup water
1 cup coconut sugar
¼ cup hibiscus tea or dried flowers
4 teaspoons pink peppercorn

ADD all of the ingredients to a saucepan and bring to a boil over medium heat. Stir until the sugar has dissolved. Remove from the heat and let steep for 20 minutes.

STRAIN into a glass jar and store in the refrigerator for up to 2 weeks.

DATE SYRUP `MAKES 1 CUP`

Date syrup retains its vitamins, minerals, antioxidants, and amino acids for a more nutritious natural sweetener.

8 dates deseeded and chopped
3 cups water

ADD the dates and the water to a saucepan and simmer over medium heat. Simmer for 30 minutes, stirring occasionally. Remove from the heat and let cool.

MOVE to a blender or food processor and blend until smooth.

TRANSFER to a glass jar and store in the refrigerator for up to 1 month.

SAKURA SYRUP MAKES 2 CUPS

One of Japan's most-cherished customs, the *hanami* (cherry blossom festival) has become a worldwide springtime event that is celebrated with rituals, teas, and cocktails. The fragrant blooms, *sakura*, make a beautiful, subtle, and unique syrup—a delicious, delicate sweetener that tastes as good on pancakes as it does in drinks.

¼ cup cherry blossom
    tea
1 cup boiling water
1 cup coconut sugar

STEEP the tea in the boiling water for 15 minutes to make a strong infusion.

ADD the tea and sugar to a saucepan and bring to a boil over medium heat. Stir until the sugar dissolves.

STRAIN into a glass jar and store in the refrigerator for up to 2 weeks.

PERSIMMON SYRUP `MAKES 2 CUPS`

The persimmon—a delicious, exotic fruit that is very high in vitamins, minerals, and organic compounds—can be eaten fresh, dried, raw, or cooked. I most enjoy them in their fresh, natural state, but since the season for persimmons is short-lived, I also love preserving the sweet and pulpy fruit in the form of a tasty syrup. Make sure to choose the Fuyu variety, which is naturally less astringent, or pick fully ripened Hachiya varieties to avoid the often bitter tannins.

2 ripe Fuyu persimmons, chopped
1 cup maple syrup
1 cup water
1-inch strip orange peel

ADD all of the ingredients to a saucepan and bring to a boil over medium heat. Stir until the syrup dissolves. Remove from the heat and let steep for 15 minutes.

STRAIN into a glass jar and store in the refrigerator for up to 2 weeks.

GINGER SYRUP

MAKES 2 CUPS

There's nothing quite like the fresh kick of ginger. With loads of medicinal properties, the spicy root has been used the world over in culinary and medical applications to reduce nausea, improve blood-sugar levels, and diminish inflammation. It is especially welcome as a delightful contrast to sweeter flavors such as chocolate, peaches, and tropical fruits.

½ cup ginger, peeled and thinly sliced
1 cup coconut sugar
1 cup water

ADD all of the ingredients to a saucepan and bring to a boil over medium-low heat. Stir until the sugar dissolves and then let simmer uncovered for 15 minutes. Remove from heat and let cool.

STRAIN into a glass jar and store in the refrigerator for up to 2 weeks.

You can easily substitute the ginger in this recipe for other spices, such as cinnamon bark or whole cloves, to create different spiced syrups.

BUTTERFLY PEA AND LAVENDER SYRUP `MAKES 1 CUP`

For drinks in magical shades of blue, violet, and pink, look no further than this butterfly pea and lavender syrup. A native plant of Southeast Asia, the beautiful butterfly pea flower has long been used in Asian culinary creations for its ability to turn food and drinks blue, and to transform into hues of purple and pink when mixed with citrus. The vibrant blue flower can be found online in dried and powdered form. Lavender adds an additional fragrant element to this lovely syrup.

1 cup coconut sugar

1 cup water

1 tablespoon dried butterfly pea flowers

1 tablespoon dried lavender

ADD all of the ingredients to a saucepan and bring to a boil over medium-high heat. Stir until the sugar dissolves. Remove from the heat and let steep for 15 minutes.

STRAIN into a glass jar and store in the refrigerator for up to 2 weeks.

SWEET PEA SYRUP `MAKES 1 CUP`

This deep verdant syrup brings out all the sweetness of the snap pea while enhancing its bright, vegetal quality. It is sure to bring a little spring into your glass.

1 cup honey
1 cup water
½ cup fresh sugar
   snap peas

ADD all of the ingredients to a saucepan and bring to a boil over medium-high heat. Stir until the honey dissolves. Remove from the heat and let steep for 15 minutes.

STRAIN into a glass jar and store in the refrigerator for up to 2 weeks.

SAFFRON ROSE SYRUP `MAKES 1 CUP`

A popular Persian flavor pairing, saffron and rose create a delicate yet intoxicating syrup that can be used in cocktails and desserts alike.

1 cup honey
1 cup water
¼ cup dried roses
20 saffron threads

ADD all of the ingredients to a saucepan and bring to a boil over medium-high heat. Stir until the honey dissolves. Remove from the heat and let steep for 15 minutes.

STRAIN into a glass jar and store in the refrigerator for up to 2 weeks.

HONEYDEW SYRUP MAKES 1 CUP

Very few flavors are as reminiscent of summer as the sweet, ripe, honeydew melon. Try this fresh melon syrup in Italian sodas, over shaved ice, and added to numerous low- and nonalcoholic cocktails to get the taste of summer any time of year.

1 honeydew melon
1 cup water
1 cup coconut sugar

PEEL and deseed the melon and cut into chunks. Put into a food processor or blender and blitz until smooth. Strain the puree through a sieve into an airtight container and set aside.

ADD the water and sugar to a saucepan and bring to a boil over medium heat. Stir until the sugar dissolves. Remove from the heat.

POUR the syrup into container with the melon mixture and stir well. Store in the refrigerator for up to 4 days.

You can easily substitute the honeydew in this recipe for other melons, such as cantaloupe, watermelon, or whatever you have on hand.

MINT DEMERARA SYRUP

MAKES 1 CUP

A popular sugar used in craft cocktail bars, demerara is a less processed form of raw cane sugar that maintains natural molasses. Simple syrup made with demerara sugar creates a richer, more complex syrup with caramel and toffee notes. The addition of mint brings a cool, refreshing pop of freshness to the syrup that will enhance a mojito and an iced tea alike.

¼ cup mint
1 cup demerara sugar
1 cup water

ADD all of the ingredients to a saucepan and bring to a boil over medium-high heat. Stir until the sugar dissolves. Remove from the heat and let steep for 15 minutes.

STRAIN into a glass jar and store in the refrigerator for up to 2 weeks.

OLEO SACCHARUM–INFUSED LEMON JUICE 1 CUP

A sustainable use of the citrus peels, oleo saccharum is an early 19th-century technique that was often used to flavor punches. The process involves using sugar to extract the oils from citrus peels, adding complex aroma and flavor to ice teas or cocktails. Here, the oleo saccharum is reintegrated with lemon juice to infuse the juice with more intense flavor.

3 whole lemons
¾ ounce sugar

PEEL the lemons and place the peels in a bowl. Add the sugar to the peels, stir well, and let infuse overnight.

JUICE the peeled lemons and set the juice aside until the lemon peels are ready.

ADD the lemon juice to the lemon peels and whisk together.

STRAIN the liquid into a glass jar and store in the refrigerator for up 3 days.

ORGEAT `MAKES 5 CUPS`

Best known as an ingredient in a mai tai and other tiki drinks, orgeat actually has French origins. The term *orge* comes from the French word for barley, and that's precisely what it was made from. Along the way, almonds were added for taste, and then at some point, people realized that besides the creamy texture, barley didn't offer much in terms of flavor and so was omitted altogether. These days, all you need to make your own orgeat are almonds and sugar.

2 cups raw almonds, sliced or chopped
1½ cups sugar
1¼ cups water
1 teaspoon orange flower water
1 ounce vodka

TOAST the almonds at 400°F for 4 minutes. Let cool. In a food processor or blender, lightly pulse the almonds until they are coarsely ground.

ADD the sugar and water to a saucepan and simmer over medium heat, stirring constantly, until the sugar dissolves. Add the almonds and simmer over low heat, continuing to stir, without bringing to boil. Remove from the heat, cover, and let infuse for an hour.

STRAIN the mixture through three layers of cheesecloth into a bowl, squeezing the cloth as you go. Add the orange flower water and vodka and mix. Store in a glass jar in the refrigerator for up to 2 weeks.

EDIBLE FLOWER
ICE CUBES MAKES 12 LARGE CUBES

Adding these cubes is an easy way to dress up your glass. They can be used in any light-colored drink for the most visual appeal.

2 extra-large ice cube trays
Distilled water, boiled and cooled
12 edible flowers

FILL the ice cube trays about one-third full with the distilled water, add a flower facing down to each cube, and freeze. Once frozen, fill the rest of the cubes with the distilled water and freeze again.

CHERRY AND BITTER
ORANGE LIQUEUR
ICE CUBES MAKES 12 SMALL CUBES

For a fun get-together, simply make a large batch of these crimson ice cubes and put out some bubbly for guests to make their own spritzes. The dark crimson ice cubes create a layered "sunrise" effect in in your drinks.

1 cup cherry juice
½ cup bitter orange liqueur
1 ice cube tray

MIX together the cherry juice and liqueur. Fill the ice cube tray with the cherry and liqueur mixture and freeze for 4 to 6 hours.

KIWI ICE CUBES MAKES 12 SMALL ICE CUBES

Kiwi brings out the fresh fruit and green notes in your clean, crisp white wines. Blending kiwi fruit with your wine and freezing them into ice cubes, adds an additional dimension to your drink without watering it down.

2 kiwi
½ cup white wine
1 ice cube tray

CUT open the kiwi and scoop out the flesh. Add the flesh and wine to a blender and blitz until smooth.

POUR the mixture into the ice cube tray and freeze for 6 to 8 hours.

RASPBERRY, ROSE, AND CHOCOLATE BIANCO VERMOUTH MAKES 750 ML

This vermouth takes your drinks to a whole new dimension. Simply substitute this infused version anytime a recipe calls for the sweeter bianco vermouth.

2 cups raspberries
¼ cup cacao nibs
¼ cup dried rose petals
1 (750 ml) bottle bianco vermouth

COMBINE the ingredients in a glass jar and allow to infuse in the refrigerator for 4 to 8 hours, or longer depending on your taste. Shake periodically to distribute flavors.

STRAIN the mixture into a clean glass jar and store in the refrigerator for up to 1 month.

TOASTED SESAME–INFUSED BIANCO VERMOUTH

MAKES 750 ML

Tiny and oil-rich, sesame seeds are one of the oldest cultivated crops in the world. According to Assyrian legend, the gods drank wine made from sesame seeds. The following infusion continues the tradition, adding the delicate, nuttiness of the prized seed to mingle with the sweet bianco vermouth for an earthy, sweet cocktail mixer to favor the gods.

1 cup white sesame seeds

1 (750 ml) bottle bianco vermouth

HEAT a large frying pan over low heat, add the sesame seeds, and toast for 3 minutes until golden brown. Remove from the heat and allow to cool.

ADD the toasted seeds to the vermouth in a glass jar and allow to infuse in the refrigerator for 4 to 8 hours, or longer depending on your taste. Shake periodically to distribute flavors.

STRAIN the mixutre into a clean glass jar and store in the refrigerator for up to 1 month.

PECAN-INFUSED SHERRY

MAKES 750 ML

Sweet, savory sherry balances cocktails wonderfully. Take the fortified wine to new heights with this nutty pecan infusion. Wild pecans were a staple of Native Americans who used to ferment pecan powder into a drink they called *powcohicora*. Loaded with antioxidants and plant-based compounds, America's native nut lends its sweet, buttery flavor to create this deliciously unique infusion.

1 cup pecans
1 tablespoon maple syrup
1 teaspoon nutmeg
1 teaspoon cinnamon powder
1 orange zest
1 (750 ml) bottle Amontillado or Olorosso sherry

SOAK the pecans in a bowl of water for 30 minutes to remove any bitterness. Meanwhile, preheat the oven to 350°F.

SPREAD the pecans on a baking sheet. Pour the maple syrup on the pecans and sprinkle with the nutmeg, cinnamon, and orange zest and mix to combine. Toast the pecans in the preheated oven for about 10 minutes, or until lightly browned. Remove from the oven and let cool.

ADD the pecans and sherry to a glass jar and let sit in the refrigerator for 4 to 8 hours, or longer depending on your taste. Shake periodically to distribute flavors.

STRAIN the mixture into a clean glass jar and and store in the refrigerator for up to 1 month.

SPRUCE-INFUSED LILLET BLANC `MAKES 750 ML`

Another native plant of North America, spruce is a striking evergreen tree with vibrant flavors and aromas. Spruce tips—the new growth of the tree—are tender, bright, and pack a citrusy punch that lends itself extremely well to infusions.

1 (750 ml) bottle of Lillet Blanc
1 cup spruce or Douglas fir needles

COMBINE the ingredients in a glass jar and let sit in the refrigerator for 4 to 8 hours, or longer depending on your taste. Shake periodically to distribute flavors.

STRAIN the mixture into a clean glass jar and store in the refrigerator for up to 1 month.

CHAI-INFUSED STOLEN RUM `MAKES 750 ML`

With notes of cinnamon, cardamom, ginger, and cloves, chai will warm your morning beverages and cocktails. Because tea can turn bitter when steeped for too long, check on this infusion every 30 minutes for best results.

2 tablespoons chai tea
1 (750 ml) bottle Stolen Smoked Rum

COMBINE the ingredients in a glass jar and let steep for about 1 hour.

STRAIN the mixture into a clean glass jar and store in the refrigerator for up to 1 month.

CANDY CAP MUSHROOM VERJUS INFUSION `MAKES 750 ML`

Only in season for 2 weeks per year, dried candy cap mushrooms release an amino acid that takes on the flavor of browned butter and maple syrup.

1 ounce dried candy
cap mushrooms
1 (750 ml) bottle
Noble Verjus

PLACE the ingredients in a large glass jar. Allow to infuse for 1 week.

STRAIN into the clean Noble Verjus bottle and store in the refrigerator for up to 1 month.

BLACK PEPPER TINCTURE

`MAKES 6 OUNCES`

A key component of traditional herbal medicine, tinctures are alcohol- or vinegar-based extracts that have been around for millennia. The alcohol or vinegar pulls out the active ingredients in the plant matter (bark, berries, leaves, roots) to concentrate them in liquid form. A black pepper tincture adds spice and dimension to your cocktail while taming bitter notes.

6 ounces vodka
2 ounces whole black
peppercorns

PLACE the ingredients in a glass jar. Allow to infuse for 2 days.

STRAIN into a clean glass jar and store in the refrigerator for up to 1 month.

ROSE WINE

MAKES 750 ML

China made the first true flower wine from chrysanthemums during the Han Dynasty. The Romans, as early as the late 4th and early 5th century, flavored wines using honey, spices, and flowers (such as the rose-infused Rosatum and the violet-infused Violatium). Since then, countless home wine crafters in Europe and colonial America have created natural wines from dandelions, elderflowers, and roses. Now, so can you. Any variety of rose can be used to infuse this wine, but please stay away from commercial brands that spray their roses with chemicals.

1 cup dried rose petals

1 (750 ml) bottle dry rosé

¼ cup cognac

¼ cup honey

COMBINE the rose petals, rosé, and cognac in a glass jar and let sit in the refrigerator for 7 days. Shake periodically to distribute flavors.

STRAIN into a clean glass jar, add the honey, and stir to combine. Let sit in the refrigerator for an additional 5 to 7 days before enjoying.

SERVE chilled and store in the refrigerator for up to 1 month.

BERRY WINE

Herbs and spices have always played an important role in the preparation of alcoholic beverages. They were added to wines, beers, and other drinks as flavoring and preservative agents as well as for their medicinal properties. One of the most ancient examples is wormwood wine, a bitter elixir prepared by steeping wormwood in wine, the direct precursor to vermouth (*vermut* is the German word for "wormwood").

Another old digestive drink was a cordial wine known as *hippocras*. Made by infusing spices in wine sweetened with honey, its name is derived from the Old French name for the Greek physician Hippocrates. The following berry wine is my updated version of Jerry Thomas' Hypocras framboise, a raspberry wine recipe that appears in his *Bar-Tender's Guide* of 1862.

1 cup raspberries
1 cup strawberries
2 tablespoons honey
¼ cup orange liqueur
1 (750 ml) bottle pinot
   noir

MUDDLE the berries in a 1-liter glass jar. Add the honey, liqueur, and wine. Cover, shake to mix, and let sit in the refrigerator for 1 week. Shake periodically to distribute flavors.

STRAIN the mixture into a clean glass jar and store in the refrigerator for up to 1 month.

ABSINTHE BITTERS MAKES 2 OUNCES

Bitters flavor cocktails the way salt and spices season food. Because premium absinthe is a robust and flavorful blend of herbs, a few drops can go a long way. Season cautiously using a small glass dropper bottle.

1 ounce Peychaud's bitters

1 ounce St. George Spirits Absinthe

ADD the ingredients to a 2-ounce dropper bottle and shake to combine.

STORE in a cool, dry place and shake well before using.

FIVE-SPICE BITTERS MAKES 6½ OUNCES

Bitters add aromatic complexity to your cocktail. This heavily spiced variety is as unique as the cocktails you'll create with it.

5 ounces vodka

2 tablespoons fennel seeds

2 teaspoons Sichuan peppercorns

1½ teaspoons cloves

1 stick cinnamon

2 star anise

ADD the ingredients to a glass jar and let sit for a minimum of 24 hours and up to several weeks.

STRAIN into a dropper bottle and store in a cool, dry place. Shake well before using.

CHOCOLATE CHILI BITTERS MAKES 6 OUNCES

With warming chocolate and spicy undertones, try adding these bitters to the Pining for Chai Cobbler (page 47) or the Boozy Red Velvet (page 126).

2 tablespoons cacao nibs
5 cardamom pods, lightly crushed
1 dried red chili
5 ounces high-proof spirit

ADD the ingredients to a glass jar and let sit for a minimum of 24 hours and up to several weeks.

STRAIN into a dropper bottle and store in a cool, dry place. Shake well before using.

HERBES DE PROVENCE SALT MAKES 2 1/2 CUPS

Why should margaritas have all the fun with salts? Try this lovely aromatic blend with the Garden Mary (page 73) and the Smoky Stalker (page 68).

1/2 cup coarse sea salt
2 cups fresh herbs, such as sage, thyme, rosemary, and small amounts of lavender

ADD the sea salt and herbs to a food processor and pulse until finely ground. Pour the salt mixture onto a baking sheet and let air dry.

TRANSFER to a glass jar and store in a cool, dry place.

HIBISCUS SALT `MAKES 1½ CUPS`

Creating a custom homemade rim salt is a lovely way to add a special touch to your drinks. Hibiscus, also known as Jamaican rose, is a beautiful flower of African origin that was first introduced to Jamaica and then to Mexico during the colonial era. It's crimson color and tart, floral taste makes it a great choice for this salt blend.

---

1 cup dried hibiscus
  flowers
½ cup sea salt

ADD the dried flowers to a blender or food processor and pulse until finely ground.

MOVE the ground flowers to a bowl, add the sea salt, and mix thoroughly.

STORE in a glass jar in a cool, dry place.

CARDAMOM SUGAR `MAKES ½ CUP`

Just like salt, sugar adds seasoning and visual appeal. This subtle yet fragrant mix will add warmth to a number of cocktails featured in this book, including as a sugar rim for the Do-Nut Fernet (page 121) or as a subtle dusting on The Tipsy Dragon (page 110).

---

10 cardamom pods
½ cup coconut sugar

CRACK open the cardamom pods and remove the seeds. Add the seeds and sugar to blender or food processor and pulse until finely ground.

STORE in a glass jar in a cool, dry place.

FERNET GLAZE `MAKES 1 CUP`

Did you know that Fernet-Branca, the rich, seductively complex bitter Italian herbal liqueur blended with 27 herbs, is just as tasty in baked goods as it is in cocktails? Use this glaze on any baked treat.

3 tablespoons Fernet-Branca
1 cup powdered sugar

WHISK the sugar and Fernet-Branca together until smooth. Use immediately.

OAT MILK `MAKES 3 CUPS`

I have shared dairy-free milk recipes in all of my previous books. They are easy to make and leave out all the unsavory additives from the store-bought versions. Oat milk, in particular, works especially well in cocktail making, thanks to its sweet, neutral taste and its light, silky texture. Here's a simple recipe to try at home.

3 cups water
1 cup rolled oats
1 whole date, pitted (optional, for sweetness, or 1 tablespoon maple syrup)
½ teaspoon vanilla extract (optional)
Pinch of salt

ADD the ingredients to a blender and blitz for about 45 seconds or until the mixture seems well combined. Do not over-blend as it can give the oat milk a slimy texture.

STRAIN the mixture through three layers of cheesecloth and transfer to a glass jar.

STORE in the refrigerator for up to 5 days.

TURMERIC SWITCHEL `MAKES 1 CUP`

Also known as "haymaker's punch," a switchel is a centuries-old drink, popularized by colonial farmers who used a combination of water, apple cider vinegar, ginger, and a sweetener to quench their thirst. With numerous health benefits, the switchel also naturally replenishes electrolytes. Turmeric brightens the mix and adds antibacterial, antiviral, and anti-inflammatory properties to the drink. Fresh turmeric looks similar to fresh ginger but is smaller and bright orange. A pinch of black pepper increases the bioavailability of turmeric's anti-inflammatory compound, curcumin. This switchel can be enjoyed over ice or added to the Solmate (page 106).

1 cup water
1 tablespoon honey
1 tablespoon apple cider vinegar
1 teaspoon grated turmeric
1 teaspoon grated ginger
½ teaspoon lemon juice
Pinch of black pepper

ADD all of the ingredients to a glass jar and let sit in the refrigerator for 6 hours or overnight.

STRAIN the mixture before drinking.

CANTALOUPE SHRUB `MAKES 2 CUPS`

Similar to a switchel, a shrub is a concentrated syrup that combines fruit, sugar, and vinegar. The result is a sweet, acidic mixer that serves the same role as citrus to provide acidity, interest, and balance to a cocktail. The use of vinegar with fruit has a long history dating back to the Babylonians and the Romans, who added fruit vinegar to water to make it safe to drink, and this practice continued throughout history.

1 cup cantaloupe

1 cup coconut sugar

1 cup champagne
    vinegar

1 teaspoon lemon zest

ADD the cantaloupe, sugar, and vinegar to a blender and blitz. Move to a glass jar and stir in the lemon zest. Cover and let sit in the refrigerator for a minimum of 4 hours and up to 2 days.

STRAIN into a clean glass jar and store in the refrigerator for up to 3 weeks.

TOMATO BASIL WATER MAKES 3 CUPS

The classic combination of tomato and basil in a unique recipe.

6 beefsteak tomatoes
½ ounce basil leaves
1 ounce white vinegar
Pinch of freshly
   cracked black
   pepper
Pinch of Maldon sea
   salt or any flaky
   sea salt

ADD all of the ingredients to a blender or food processor and pulse gently until well blended.

STRAIN the mixture through three layers of cheesecloth into a glass jar and store in the refrigerator for 3 to 4 days.

CRANBERRY MORS `MAKES 4 CUPS`

Cranberry Mors is a tart berry sipper that's better than any sugary sweet cranberry juice on the market. And thankfully, you can even make it at home. If you don't have cranberries, get creative and swap them out for red currants, gooseberries, or lingonberries.

2 cups cranberries
4 cups water
Honey to taste

ADD the ingredients to a large saucepan and cook on medium high heat. Bring to a boil and allow the mixture to simmer for 15 minutes. Remove from the heat and let cool.

STRAIN into a glass container and keep refrigerated for up to one week.

low-ABV BOTTLES TO KNOW

The following is a list of high-quality, low-proof alcohols that are often used to build and flavor low-ABV cocktails. They are listed by category here for easy reference.

FRUIT LIQUEURS

CHERRY: Brands include Denmark's Cherry Heering, Italy's Luxardo Maraschino, and the United States's Leopold Bros.

CRÈME DE CASSIS: Blackcurrant liqueur, most classically used in the kir and kir royale cocktails.

ORANGE: This category includes liqueurs like triple sec and curaçao; consider brands such as Combier and Leopold Bros.

PEACH: Mathilde Peach.

PEAR (SPICED): St. George Spirits, Poire Williams, Pür•Spirits.

RASPBERRY: St. George Spirits.

SLOE GIN: Liqueur made from sloeberries.

FLORAL LIQUEURS

CRÈME DE VIOLETTE: Purple-hued, violet-flavored liqueur.

ITALICUS ROSOLIO DI BERGAMOTTO: An Italian Bergamot liqueur that features rose, gentian, lavender, and chamomile among its ingredients. This liqueur is technically part of the amaro-adjacent category of rosolio—liqueurs with rose water in their recipes.

ST-GERMAIN: Elderflower-flavored liqueur.

COFFEE AND CHOCOLATE LIQUEURS

CACAO: Try the offerings by Giffard.

COFFEE: Coffee-flavored liqueur by brands such as St. George Spirits.

HERBAL AND SPICED LIQUEURS

AVERNA: Intensely sweet and flavorful, made of roughly 60 ingredients that are macerated and infused in a neutral spirit.

BENEDICTINE: French herbal liqueur.

BECHEROVKA: A spicy clove and cinnamon–laced Czech liqueur.

BRÀULIO: Distinct with pine-like taste, closely linked to its Alpine origins of Bormio. Made from 13 different herbs and ingredients found in the Valtellina mountain region of Italy.

CAMPARI/APEROL: Campari is more intense, with strong orange hints, a bitter taste, and viscous texture. Aperol is softer, with a lower ABV. For a more authentic, small batch experience, consider St. Agrestis made in New York or Pür•Spirits orange liqueur made in California.

CHARTREUSE: A French brandy-based herbal liqueur, originally made in a monastery outside of Paris and based on a recipe nicknamed the "Elixir of Long Life."

> **Green Chartreuse**: Made with 130 herbs and plants, and it's the only liqueur in the world that is naturally green.

> **Yellow Chartreuse**: Milder and sweeter than its green counterpart.

CYNAR: Cynar is made from a variety of herbs and ingredients, but it's best known for being made with artichokes.

DRAMBUIE: Scotch whisky–based liqueur made with honey, herbs, and spices.

FERNET-BRANCA: A dark, herbaceous liqueur made with a myriad of herbs and spices including myrrh, rhubarb, chamomile, cardamom, aloe, and saffron. A favorite behind the bar, Fernet is often referred to as "the bartender's handshake."

GAMMEL DANSK BITTER DRAM: Denmark's version of an amaro, featuring 29 ingredients including gentian root, coriander, wormwood, and China bark, whch make a moderately bitter tipple.

MELETTI/RAMAZZOTTI: Amari made from the kola nut.

MONTENEGRO: Amaro from Italy with 40 botanicals including orange peel, coriander, nutmeg, marjoram, cloves, and cinnamon.

NONINO: An Italian grappa-based amaro aged in *barrique* (small sherry casks) that are made in Nevers, France.

PINEAU DES CHARENTES: An apéritif made by blending cognac and grape must.

POMP & WHIMSY: A unique gin-based liqueur.

RIGA BLACK BALSAM: A Latvian tipple made of 17 herbs, roots, and grasses that are infused in neutral spirits and then blended with honey, juices, and other ingredients.

ZUCCA RABARBARO: A distinct infusion with subtle bitterness and smokiness made by smoking Chinese rhubarb stems.

LICORICE AND ANISE LIQUEURS

Aguardiente from Colombia

Herbsaint from the United States

Jägermeister from Germany

Ouzo from Greece

Pernod or anisette from France

Raki from Turkey

Sambuca from Italy

ALCOHOL PERCENTAGE IN DRINKS

The legal categories for alcohol are beer, wine, and spirits, but there are many subcategories and the ABV of each varies extensively.

BEERS (3 TO 10%)

Pilsner: 3 to 6%

ESB (Bitter): 3 to 6%

Lager: 4 to 5%

Porter: 4 to 5%

Brown ale: 4 to 6%

IPA (India Pale Ale): 6 to 7%

Stout: 5 to 10%

WINES (8 TO 14%)

Sparkling wine: 8 to 12%

Table wine: 9 to 14%

Dry white wine: 10 to 12%

Red wine: 11 to 14%

Barley wine: 11 to 15%

FORTIFIED WINES (16 TO 22%)

Marsala wine: 15 to 17%

Madeira wine: 15 to 18%

Vermouth: 15 to 18%

Port wine: 16 to 20%

Sherry: 17 to 22%

SPIRITS (20 TO 70%)

Light liqueurs: 15 to 25%

Vodka: 40 to 95%

Gin: 36 to 50%

Rum: 36 to 50%

Whiskey: 36 to 50%

Tequila: 50 to 51%

Mezcal: 40 to 55%

Cask-strength whiskey: 60%

Absinthe: 55 to 90%

Neutral grain spirits: 95%

Rectified spirits: 96%

Absolute alcohol: 96 to 98%

resources

COCKTAIL MIXERS

Andtonic.co

Artisanal tonic syrup

Alteyaorganics.com

Organic rose water

My.doterra.com/julesaron

CPTG-certified pure, therapeutic-grade, organic, edible essential oils

Fever-tree.com

Organic sodas, tonic water, ginger beer

Gourmetfoodstore.com

Extensive collection of gourmet staples, including exotic pantry items and spices

Inpursuitoftea.com

Large assortment of loose-leaf teas, blends, and tea accessories.

Justdatesyrup.com

Pure date syrup and pomegranate syrup

Lalunasalt.com

Infused gourmet sea salts

Lilyofthedesert.com

Organic aloe vera juice

Drinkmonday.co

Zero-alcohol gin

Orgeatworks.com

Toasted nut orgeat syrups

Qtonic.com

Organic sodas

Seedlipdrinks.com/us

Nonalcoholic spirits

Simplyorganic.com

Spices, crystallized ginger, Madagascar Bourbon vanilla beans

Southmatea.com

Artisan custom tea blends

Sipsongspirits.com

Tea that tastes like gin!

Wildhibiscus.com

Syrups

BAR AND KITCHEN TOOLS

Bevmo.com

Barware

Thebostonshaker.com

Barware

Cocktailkingdom.com

Barware

Crateandbarrel.com

Glassware

Canningfresh.com

Sealable glass jars

Cuisinart.com

Quality blenders

Glassdharma.com

Reusable glass drinking straws

Riedel.com

Quality glassware

Pyrex.com

Jars, glassware, storage
   containers

Oxo.com

Ice cube trays with lids

Sempli.com

Designer glassware

Surlatable.com

Jars, glassware, kitchen tools

Surfsidesips.com

Glass straws

Tovolo.com

BPA-free silicon ice cube trays

Vitamix.com

High-speed blenders

SUPERFOODS

Animamundi.com

Herbal and superfood blends

Mountainroseherbs.com

Culinary and medicinal herbs
   and spices

Navitasorganics.com

Organic superfoods such as
   cacao powder, chia seeds,
   goji berries, and wheatgrass
   powder

Moodbeli.com

Adaptogen and botanical blends

Rootandbones.com

Specializes in organic medicinal
   mushrooms

Sambazon.com

Specializes in acai products

Nutrex-Hawaii.com

Specializes in spirulina

Frontiercoop.com

Dried herbs, seasonings, and
   extracts

EDUCATIONAL RESOURCES

Eatrightamerica.com
Great organization providing information on superfoods and the ANDI chart

Forksoverknives.com
Info on preventing disease by including more plant-based whole foods

Thehealthybartender.com
Better-for-you cocktail recipes that include full-proof, low-ABV, and nonalcoholic drinks made with healthy ingredients and no refined sugar

acknowledgments

The Low-Proof Happy Hour marks my fifth book to date, and my gratitude runs deep for the continued opportunity to share my passion for wellness with so many of you. Thank you, dear reader, for enjoying, supporting, and sharing my books. May you find inspiration and guidance in these pages to keep your glass full for years to come.

To Dylan, for keeping my own cup full and for remaining my best and most enthusiastic taste tester throughout the years.

To my mom, for reminding me to stay nourished with delicious care packages throughout my endless editing periods.

To my dad, for your abundance of knowledge, advice, and persistent reminders to stay strong and do right.

To my darling girlfriends Liz, Corie, Pamela, Judie, and Shani, who even so many miles away, remind me of what true friendship and support really feel like. I'm hardly great at staying in touch, but you are forever in my hearts.

It takes masterful individuals to produce meaningful books, and I have been lucky to have two incredible constants throughout my publishing journey: Marilyn Allen and Ann Treistman, thank you both for taking a chance on me when all I had was an intention and a book title. Here we are five books later!

To the many contributors, my deepest gratitude for sharing your talent, knowledge, and inspiration. A special thank you to John Picard, Natalie Migliarini, Jillian Vose, Matthew Biancaniello, Warren Bobrow, Jason Yu, Eric Vincent, Cat Shell, Lukas B. Smith, Alyssa Sartor, Frankie Rodriguez, Giorgia Crea, Louis Peressin, Peter Siewruk, Emma Kuhl Matthew Rose, Charlie Shapiro, Dr. Nicola Nice, Dustin Bolinis, Cassidy Moser, Keith Popejoy, Walter Johnson, Summer-Jane Bell, Will Benedetto, Lily Jenson, Taylor Amos.

And finally, to the hardworking Countryman Press team, thank you for the heaping spoonful of dedication poured into this book.

I am forever beholden.

recipe credits

Recipe and art for Godzilla (page 146) by Jillian Vose
Recipe for Can't Elope (page 149) by Lily Jensen
Recipe and art for Shochu 50/50 (page 150) by Jason Yu
Recipe for Shift Break (page 153) by Eric Vincent
Recipe for Santa Rosa (page 154) by cocktail chef, Eat Your Drink
Recipe for Sizzle Reel Sangaree (page 157) by Lukas Smith
Recipe for The Stolen Moon (page 158) by Alyssa Laura Sartor,
    proprietor of August Laura
Recipe for Green Light (page 161) by Giorgia Crea
Recipe and art for All Night Long (page 162) by Pete Siewruk
Recipe for Borrowing From Others in Time (page 165) by
    Warren Bobrow
Recipe for Oaxaca Grace (page 166) by Matthew Rose
Recipe for Hollywood to Houston (page 169) Charlie Shapiro
Recipe for Breakfast in Tokyo (page 170) by Nicola Nice
Recipe for Guanalope (page 173) by Dustin Bolin
Recipe for Jaunito Amor (page 174) by Casidy Moser
Recipe for Sangrito (page 177) by Keith Popejoy
Recipe for Dubonnet Spritz (page 178) by Walter Johnson
Recipe for Far Eastside (page 181) by Frank Alessio
Recipe for Pacific Crest Trail (page 182) by Summer-Jane Bell
Recipe for Caprese Cooler (page 185) by Will Benedetto

index

© Francesca | Coviello Photo

ABOUT THE AUTHOR

Named "the wellness mixologist" by *Women's Health* magazine, Jules is the beverage consultant and holistic nutritionist bridging the gap between mind, body, and spirit(s) for over a decade. She is the founder of The Healthy Bartender, the online clean cocktail destination.

Jules is the author of five best-selling books, including the acclaimed cocktail book, *Zen and Tonic*.

When she's not writing, Jules works as a beverage consultant; serves as the beverage director for the annual Seed Food and Wine Festival held in Miami, Los Angeles, and Brooklyn; and works with the nonprofit Lox Farm dinners in Palm Beach, raising funds for their "food as medicine" Fresh Rx program. She is a regular nutrition expert on WPTV, serves on the United States Bartender's Guild health and wellness committee, and is *Thrive* magazine's bartender in residence.

Jules has been featured in *Forbes*, *HuffPost*, *New York Post*, *Imbibe*, *Goop*, and *Elle*; appeared on *The Today Show*; and is a regular contributor to *Thrive*, *Women's Health*, mindbodygreen, *Organic Spa*, and *Woman's World*, among other national outlets.